Looking through

Gramsci's eyes:

Correcting what everyone overlooked

"*the school as the positive educative function, and the courts as a repressive and negative educative function, are the most important State activities*" Antonio Gramsci

Unedited version

Kevin Mitanidis

Copyright 2018 by Kevin Mitanidis

All Rights Reserved

All rights reserved. No part of this publication may be reproduced or transmitted in any form or by any means, electronically, or mechanically, including photocopy, recording, or by any information storage and retrieving system without permission from the publisher.

For further information or request for permission to make copies of any part of the work should be written form and mailed to the following address.

To contact us:

e-mail kmgramsci@gmail.com

Looking through Gramsci's eyes

First edition 2018. Printed in USA.

ISBN 978-1-7753259-0-1

Looking through Gramsci's eyes

DEDICATION

To my son, who must always remember that when you have become a Physician and people ask you why you chose this profession, just tell them because my daddy told me too. If you forget I will constantly remind you.

CONTENTS

	Acknowledgments	i
	Abstract	1
	Introduction	2
1	What others have contributed to Gramsci's theory of hegemony	3
2	The law and the courts my contribution begins	12
3	The Canadian court system	34
4	Reference question an instrument of legal coercion	40
5	Raising the level of civilizing in the interests of the ruling class	65
6	Coercion and the *Charter*	85
7	ADR and the pressures within the superstructure	105
8	The Nation State	117
	Conclusion	130
	Bibliography	135
	Cases cited	140

ACKNOWLEDGMENTS
Alfa and Omega

My son Ethan who sat on my lap, at a young age, while this was being written.

My partner, Paola...

Dad and Mom.

To Professor Owen Fiss of Yale Law School. In recognition of your inspiration and kind words over our correspondence. An honor.

To Professor Michael Mandel of Osgood Hall Law School who has since passed on, your work will continue to inspired many. Who always had a good lawyer joke on hand for every class.

To Professor Radha Persaud Of York University. A person who has aided in the development of so many young minds. You are appreciated

To Professor Denise Pilon of the Political Science Department at York University. Your insights and encouragement. Much appreciated

To Professor Heather MacRae of the Political Science department at York University. For hanging in there, and your support. Much appreciated.

To Professor Richard Haigh of Osgood Hall York University. Your support. Much appreciated.

To Professor Esteve Morera of the Political science and Philosophy Departments at York University. Last but not least, my supervisor. Has been my honor.

Abstract:

It is a common misunderstanding among many scholars that Antonio Gramsci said very little about the law. To the contrary, not only did Gramsci write with extensive knowledge of the law and the legal systems of his day, but he illustrated how the law operates as a tool for the coercive purposes of the ruling class. The reader of the Prison Notebooks must look at the entire collection as one complete theory of hegemony. Every word and every idea of Gramsci's writings fits into a cleverly crafted concept of what he meant his theory of hegemony to represent.

Introduction:

Antonio Gramsci is known, from his insights into the relationships of domination within the state, by his theory of hegemony. Gramsci developed his theory of hegemony as a result of attempting to understand what made the mass population willingly consent to what he described as the oppression by those that controlled the means of production or the ruling class. It was the aim of his writing to invoke thought in those who read his work about the world around them and I, invite you to do the same. The state, for Gramsci, is a conceptualization of the superstructure and the base structures. The superstructure comprises two spheres, one of civil society and the other of political society. Each interact with the states base economic structure. Government, located in the sphere of political society, represented by individuals who Gramsci describes as intellectuals, serve to further the ideology of the dominant social group. Civil society, representing the second sphere of the superstructure, having its own set of institutions is also represented by various people or intellectuals in institutional positions that support this same dominant ideology of the dominant social group. The dominant social group or ruling class control the modes of production and need a functional system of governance within the state to be able to maintain the obedience to their leadership. All of these institutions as Gramsci explains, interact together to support the ruling class, who ultimately lead to maintain ideologically subservience of individual subgroups within the nation state. So, it's not just money that makes the world function but obedience to a dominant ideology according to Gramsci. This book will provide a complete picture of how Gramsci envisioned his theory of hegemony, including mention of the legal system for which no proper discussion of hegemony can be without. Through an illustration of the Canadian system it will be evident that his theory is applicable today, just over eighty years after his death. It is a very simple closed system that Gramsci envisions of the state, purposively designed to keep the dominant social group in their position of power or to maintain their hegemony. Gramsci's aim, as is mine in illustrating his theorizations, is to open dialogue and debate by capturing the reader's attention to awaken them to their surroundings that they may arrive at a philosophy of praxis.

Chapter one:
What others have contributed to Gramsci's theory of hegemony

Coercive and non-coercive institutional forces are the two main forces within the superstructure that interact together in support of maintaining organized consent or hegemony[1]. The coercive forces of the state, representing such institutions as the courts, are used to gain consent to supporting the hegemony of the dominant social group or ruling class. Most of the institutional forces of ideological production such as social media, schools, churches, etc., which exist within civil society that function to secure the willingness of the mass population to comply with the interests of the dominant social group in a continuous web of interaction. According to Gramsci, organized consent refers to "the spontaneous consent given by the great mass of the population to the general direction imposed on social life by the dominant fundamental group" (SPN, 12). Gramsci's theory of hegemony is supported by the concept that one dominant social group leads the mass population or all other subgroups. According to William Robinson, in his book *A Theory of Global Capitalism*, all social order is maintained through a combination of consensual and coercive dimensions; hegemony is consensus protected, in Gramsci's words, by the 'armor of coercion' (Robinson, 161)[2]. This is Robinsons

---

[1] Coercion is not meant to imply physical force and non-coercive denotes the willingness to comply. See Chapter Two, where this is illustrated.

[2] It seems that Robinson may have been utilizing the word coercion to include physical force, when referencing Gramsci. While there are institutional forces at work within the State

interpretation of what Gramsci equates as "the state = political society + civil society, in other words hegemony protected by the armor of coercion" (SPN, 263). In large part, the coercive forces function to influence the mass population into willfully following or to consent to the leadership of the dominant social group. Douglas Litowitz, in his paper *Gramsci, Hegemony, and the Law*, describes the relationship between the coercive and non-coercive forces as complimentary to gain control over those that are dominated by the dominant social group. According to Litowitz, "it was in the *Prison Notebooks* that Gramsci developed the concept of hegemony to describe a condition in which the supremacy of a social group is achieved not only by physical force; representing the non-consensual or non-coercive forces of the superstructure (which Gramsci called "domination" or "command"), but also through consensual submission of the very people who were dominated (a phenomenon that Gramsci variously called 'leadership,' 'direction,' or 'hegemony')" (Litowitz, 518). Litowitz describes the purpose both the non-coercive or consensual element that works in joint with different coercive forces within the superstructure as intending to attain "control [that] is exercised increasingly at the level of popular belief through the dissemination of a dominant outlook" (Litowitz, 518). "This does not mean that physical

---

that use physical force to maintain compliance to the directives of leadership it should not be confused by assuming that consent is achieved through force it is only obtained by the other willing to consent and not forced. But they do protect the coercive forces through enforcement such as forcing members of society to attend court and enforce contracts in the private sector or civil society that allow these institutions to conduct their affairs in a certain manner.

force is replaced by reeducation camps but rather that control is exercised increasingly at the level of popular belief through the dissemination of a dominant outlook" (Litowitz, 524). There is a relationship of forces located within both political and civil societies that support the dominant ideology; working together to obtain control over the mass population by spreading and influencing the support of the dominant ideology of the ruling class.

It was Marx who proposed, "the dominant ideology of every society is the ideology of the dominant class" (E. Mandel, 1970). Gramsci's theory of hegemony expands upon Marx's own theorizations. According to Ernest Mandel in his paper *The Leninist Theory of Organization*, the dialectic interpretation of this means that "the ideology of the ruling class has control over the means of ideological production which society has at its disposal (the church, schools, mass media, etc.), and uses these means in its own interests" (E. Mandel, 1970). Ultimately, those that control the economical means of production lead and control the modes of ideological production within the superstructure. Duncan Kennedy, in his paper *Antonio Gramsci and the Legal System,* defines the dominant ideology of a society as almost invisible in how it works itself within all facets of the state. According to Kennedy, Gramsci "uses a concept which he calls 'historic bloc' which suggests that the meaning of a particular economic formation, and of a particular set of economic forces, is embedded in a set of economic, social, political, cultural and other ideological ideas and vice versa" (Kennedy, 34). Kennedy uses the word constellations to denote the intricate web design, how all of these forces work together invisibly, that can only be understood as an ideological concept (Kennedy, 34)[3]. According to Kennedy "Gramsci stands for the reawakening of the notion that Marxists could think seriously about, work hard on, be deeply interested in and try to figure out the mechanisms by which people are persuaded, rather than brutally coerced, into accepting a capitalist regime" (Kennedy, 32)[4]. This identifies one brilliant aspect of Gramsci's work; the ability to look into what mechanisms are at work that maintain the hold over a societies popular views[5]. According to Allan Hunt in his paper, *Rights and Social Movements: Counter Hegemonic strategies*, Gramsci had broken from the traditional Marxist conception of ideology. He describes this as a break from the "intellectual plane of philosophical systems of Marx to a formation of popular consciousness or common sense" (Hunt, 310). The most distinctive feature, according to Hunt, "of Gramsci's account of ideology was a break with Marx's conception of ideology as 'ideology', that is, as a *Weltanschauung*, a coherent world view, intellectually developed and at the same time informing the consciousness of active social classes" (Hunt, 310). This shift according to Hunt that represent "mechanisms through which participation in social life is possible" (Hunt, 310)). This participation can happen actively and passively according to Gramsci.

---

[3] It is unclear if Kennedy is using the word 'invisibility' in a way similar to that of Engels, but he seems to be using it to distinguish how the exchange of ideas among the base structure and super structure can easily go unnoticed

[4] Again, Kennedy like Robinson may be using coercion as enforcement but it is unclear from this passage.

[5] Not to be confused with the concept that this enforces the idea that knowledge is a social construct legitimizing societies structure.

Both, Kennedy and Litowitz found that Gramsci added to Marxist theory, this salient non-coercive feature within the structure of society[6]. According to Litowitz

> This brilliant addition to Marxist theory draws attention to areas neglected by Marxists as epiphenomenal (art, common sense, education, religion), but it also captures the degree to which a dominant order is reflected at multiple levels. The resulting structure (the historical bloc) forms a giant system that is internalized as 'common sense', which Gramsci saw as a ragtag and often contradictory set of basic beliefs and presuppositions that reflect the existing arrangement. The idea of a historical bloc and its internalization as a matter of common sense helps to account for the tenacity of an existing way of life. For Gramsci, domination becomes encoded at all levels of a system, resulting in a kind of multilevel homeostasis where a dominant group (or a particular class of people) controls the repressive power of the police force as well as the intellectual means of production, namely the schools, news media, entertainment, and other

---

[6] In contrast to Stephen Gill use of the term 'historic bloc' which he uses to denote a "homogenous politico-economic alliance". The term is used in this paper not as a moment of conception when social forces are starting to secure their hegemony, but in the same way it is used by Litowitz and Kennedy as simply referring to the unity of (base) structure and super structure.

mechanisms for the molding of popular culture (Litowitz, 528).

Most of the mass population believe that the government works on their behalf while it serves to support their subordinate position to those in control of the economic productive forces. According to Hunt "one of the most important corollaries Gramsci's conception of hegemony is that for a hegemonic project to be dominant it must address and incorporate, if only partially, some aspects of the aspirations, interests, and ideology of subordinate groups" (Hunt, 311). What Hunt is describing is that subgroups will only be willing to comply or be complacent with leadership if they support what they believe to be their own interests.

The way in which the mass population willfully accepts the ideology of the ruling class or consents to the coercion, is represented in three ways according to Litowitz, through universalization, naturalization and rationalization. According to Litowitz, universalization means "the dominant group manages to portray its parochial interests and obsessions as the common interests of all people. This can take place in subtle ways" (Litowitz, 525). Naturalization is "a given way of life that becomes 'reified' to the point where "culture" is confused with "nature" at every turn, which induces quietism because there is no point in fighting against nature. As for the strategy of rationalization, Gramsci points out that every ruling group gives rise to a class of intellectuals who perpetuate the existing way of life at the level of theory" (Litowitz, 526). He separates intellectuals into ordinary and functional. The functionary intellectuals exist in the institutions of both political and civil societies directly work to consciously convey the ideology of the ruling class intending to gain others acceptance to it while ordinary intellectuals support the dominant ideology are in positions within institutions and go along with the status quo but are still in positions of influence. Differences between the two types of intellectuals are not subtle because functionary intellectuals carry more influence that do ordinary intellectuals; directing others including ordinary intellectuals in how to carry or better influence of the ruling class over others. Those that promote the dominant ideology in political society, the functionary intellectuals, work to maintain the leadership of the dominant social group including politicians, and judges. Similar to Litowitz view, Kennedy finds that, the idea of hegemony "is very close to our conception of ideology. It is the notion of the exercise of domination through political legitimacy, rather than through force. Hegemony is the notion of the acquisition of the consent of the governed" (Kennedy, 1). Therefore, people rationalize that it is their interest to follow leadership. The legitimacy of government institutions is bound together with the authority that is granted to those in positions in government who control the coercive apparatus of the state including the police, military, and courts. Litowitz expounds the view that Gramsci's insights into this non-coercive element of hegemony is a complement to Marxist theory for how Gramsci has identified an almost multi-layered aspect to the structure of society. A certain standard of morality represented by a set of moral beliefs and ideologies is established within the state that is uniformly accepted as the basis for social behavior within the state. Once a certain level of moral standard or sets of ideological beliefs are adopted. which are accepted by the mass population, then they must be represented in laws and enforced by the state. Gramsci recognized the role of the law and the courts integral part in this connection. He makes brief comments in the *Prison Notebooks'* in relation to how the law and the courts, by design, are utilized to maintain social order within the state.

Chapter two:
The law and the courts my contribution begins

By regulating negative behaviors, through the creation of laws, government is engaged in civilizing. Reciprocally, certain positive behaviors are manifested and created among the mass population with the help of institutional forces within both political and civil societies in the superstructure. The function of prescribed laws is to help dictate relationships with in the state: between its individual members, between individuals and government, between different government institutions, between governments and the modes of production and finally between the individuals of the state and the modes of production[7]. According to Gramsci "civilizing [is the] activity undertaken by the state" (SPN, 247), where the state either creates "a new type or level of civilizing" (SPN, 247). Much of the state's laws, which regulate behavior, are based on certain abstract values or principles that the majority of the population supports; such as it is wrong to commit murder or to steal. Some of these values are represented in codified and un-codified constitutional law; for example, the freedom of speech that is located in the Canadian Charter of Rights and Freedoms. As in Canada, some of these values provide substance to certain laws, which ultimately began or were accepted pre-constitution as community standards. Since the twelfth century it was common that "whenever Parliament had not provided a law to define how a dispute should be settled, the courts would settle the dispute according to what the judges believed to be

---

[7] There are more relationships that may be included, such as different relationships between differing social groups but these are the main ones and I only use these for illustration.

the community standards" (Greene, 10). So, when there was no statute or common law in place, the court had in the past appealed to community standards or abstract values, which were accepted by the majority of the mass population, to resolve issues. The manner that Gramsci describes how the state civilizes illustrates that he not only understood how the law was developed but understood that most civil societies gained their acceptance of the conception of the rule of law from a development based upon this idea to adopt laws and appeal to the most widely held beliefs of the majority of society to gain consent to leadership. Once certain abstract values or principles are adopted and a level of civilizing is introduced by the state, this level of civilizing is enforced. Then, the mass population by willfully consenting to follow the law, bases their consent on how they relate to these values which certain laws are founded upon. The state then continues to build upon these foundational abstract values, replacing and adding new principles based on these values over time. This building upon values to create new laws is what Gramsci considers as the state's ability to raise the level of civilizing of the mass population and therefore to a large degree is how the state influences what becomes acceptable normal behavior in civil society. This raising level of civilizing represents the mass population manipulation of becoming more obedient to leaderships direction towards a certain type of collective society.

There are different areas of law that are more directly aimed at promoting a certain level of civilizing in the state over others, as Gramsci recognizes. Criminal law is a category of the law that is specifically designed to outline most of the unacceptable behavioral parameters of the mass population. From a philosophical stand point, criminal laws are contingent in the sense that there is no set of underlining rules on what makes a prohibited act, a criminal act. In other words, it is not mandatory that an action for it to be considered a crime to be based on any moral values and the state has the choice to simply make whatever behavior it wants a prohibited act. According to Gramsci, the conception of the law "must be an essentially innovatory one is not to be found, integrally, in any pre-existing doctrine" (SPN, 246). If the state is to create criminal law based on some set of values, then what are these values to be? There are no pre-determined set, a priori, criteria for what values certain laws are to be based upon and the creation of a moral standard is something entirely done according to the states discretion. But the state must consider that the willful acceptance of these laws is crucial for the state to function properly. It therefore appeals to certain core values in the promotion of the creation of certain laws. Gramsci in discussing the French revolution of the Napoleonic period, outlined how the bourgeoisie class brought revolution into the conception of the law, directing how the state functions. It was this idea or the idea promoted by the revolution, of change, that "created the will" of the mass population to conform to the civilizing as directed by the state (SPN, 260). A conception in the law or what idea is behind the making of a law, aids in the creation of organized consent. This is similar to how the courts appealed to community standards or to abstract values which are held by the majority of the mass population. The civilizing of the state according to Gramsci represents the "ethnicity of the law and of the state" (SPN, 260). Ethnicity or the ethical component of the law is also used by Gramsci to denote universality, which represents a widely held belief or beliefs (SPN, 259). So, consent to the law represents consent to the level of civilizing and to the abstract principles behind the law. Simply put, these values and principles of what the law is supposedly based upon represent the ethical component of the law and what is meant by its universality or its universal appeal. The consent given by the majority of the mass population to follow the law, represents consent to leadership. It is leadership that ultimately defines the law imposing a certain level of civilizing. So, certain laws are enacted and then promoted based on certain values in order for the state to build a level of civilizing in the state. In Canada, liberal ideology has often been conceptualized abstractly in the making of what underpins various laws. It is a belief in what the law represents or what abstract value it represents that aid's in the maintenance of organized consent to the level of civilizing by the state. Gramsci's concern with abstract values which underscore certain laws was to understand the general premise with how laws generally are attached to bigger issues and how these values can be manipulated or replaced to the advantage of the dominant ruling class when there interests are concerned. The role of government, that includes the courts, is to reconcile the often-opposing interests between different subgroups within the mass population with the interests of the ruling class. While not all laws have an immediate identifiable grounding in any particular value, Gramsci's concern was with the abstractness of certain values which the state could then reinterpret and build upon to raise the level of civilizing. He elaborates on the manner in which certain laws are based, making them more easily manipulated, which enables the ruling class through their intellectuals to manipulate the level of civilizing to their desired effect of obedience. For example, in Canada the promotion of liberal ideology allows for the suppression of some laws over others. This allows the interests of the ruling class to be furthered while maintaining organized consent to the direction of leadership (this will be examined in detail later in the book).

By continuously appealing to certain abstract values that are supported by the majority of the mass population, the government is actively engaged in the maintenance of organized consent. As leadership raise's the level of civilizing, the government aims to balance the interests of different subgroups against the interests of the ruling class. Specifically, when the interests of the ruling class are already supported in the law, the government, will appeal to certain abstract values to alter the level of civilizing or as Gramsci describes it as raising the level of civilizing in support of the furtherance of these interests of the ruling[8]. Laws need to be enacted, interpreted, applied and enforced by the state and it is the state that engages in influencing support or consent to their leadership through the law and the courts. This duty to influence the mass population into the direction of leadership falls on different institutions within political society but it is the legislature and the courts which are an integral part of the coercive apparatus of the state and thus a tool of the ruling class who controls government. Legal coercion and the enforcement of the law must involve the consideration of 'public opinion' in order to achieve this level of consent. To raise the level of civilizing, institutions of political society that create laws that build upon certain basic abstract values, as such the value that it is wrong to steal, creating new societal norms which often lead to the replacement of

---

[8] See Chapter five for how this is illustrated through the example of labour struggles in Canada.

old laws with new laws that are consistent with the direction of leadership and therefore the ruling class. According to Gramsci this ethical component of the law or appeal to universally accepted abstract values is a continual creation of the state (SPN, 258). For example, there is no formal debate taken up by the state to ascertain whether any criminal act is truly immoral against some epistemology but they will continue to create out of abstract appeal to certain values new laws that will alter the relationships within the state for the advantage of the ruling class. There will always be those subgroups or individuals who do not consent to some of the decisions of the government directives or to some of the values that laws are built upon. But, Gramsci was concerned with how the majority reacted to the imposed civilizing by leadership, represented by public opinion (SPN 258). This cultural climate of the majority of the mass population is measurable according to Gramsci by what the public opinion is; representing the general consensus among the majority of the mass population as to how government changes the level of civilizing. This level of civilizing, as Gramsci identifies, must be spontaneously and freely accepted and not just forced upon the mass population (SPN, 195). It is through means of legal coercion that the institutions in political society aim at obtaining organized consent to the level of civilizing imposed by the state. Enforcement of these laws and therefore the level of civilizing is taken up by the institutions in the state such as the police, guards at jails, military, etc. The coercive apparatus of political society represents the law and the courts, and it is the courts who apply laws which legally invokes the mechanisms of state enforcement institutions of political society.

Gramsci makes specific reference to criminal law in the *Prison Notebooks* to aid in his illustration of how the state civilizes. It is the prospect of state punishments that distinguishes criminal law from all other forms of law or acts or omissions that would give rise to legal proceeding. Gramsci describes the state as "[operating] according to a plan, it urges, incites, solicits, and 'punishes" (SPN, 247). For example, the state authorizes the use of legalized punishments though the criminal courts, who decide if a law has been broken and what appropriate action is to be taken by the state in accordance of the law. According to Gramsci, the "[state] should be viewed as a body that has legitimized use of force, to punish bad actions and reward "praiseworthy and meritorious activity…criminal action or omission must have a punitive sanction, with moral implication and not merely judged as dangerous" (SPN, 247). A criminal action or crime is behavior that is prohibited by the state, making the state's primary function in creating criminal law as to limit certain behavior. A criminal omission is a duty to act, imposed by the law, commanding action on the part of an individual in given circumstances. An omission is a negative freedom because it prohibits a non-action where the possibility of criminal liability may occur. Gramsci argues that criminal laws should have moral implications and does not say that all laws do. A possible correct interpretation of this is that if all criminal laws have moral implications or appealed to these widely held abstract principles, the state would not seem as if they are bureaucratized in raising the level of civility in support of the interests of the ruling class. Gramsci describes the goal of the state is to continuously adapt the "civilizing and the morality of the broadest popular masses to the necessities of the continuous development of the economic apparatus of production (SPN, 242).

Once these abstract values are incorporated in laws, government constantly appeals to these abstract values, (which can change over time as the state raises the level of civilizing) allowing government to be perceived as if they are always civilizing in support of the needs of the mass population. It is the act of building upon these abstract values or principles, through the creation of new laws or a re-interpretation of these principles that enables government to raise the level of civilizing. And, one main concern of how the level is to be raised is so that the mass population or their behavior will support the economic system of the state.

By prohibiting behavior, the state is directly influencing how the mass population organizes their behaviors and relationships within the state institutions. All laws, whether they are restrictive to a particular segment of the mass population or apply to everyone, they are imposed and are therefore coercive by nature in how leadership must gain the mass populations consent to follow the law. Gramsci, describes that consent to the law is achieved by "turning necessity or what individuals feel that they need along with some form of coercion, that may include the law, then changing these 'into freedom' and this is achieved [this transformation of the mass population into a collective man] through the law" (SPN, 242). The mass population is placed in the position of adapting their current level of civilizing and system of beliefs to what behaviors are acceptable or what positive freedoms that they choose to experience while they peruse a way of life within the state. The law in general is described by Gramsci as the "repressive and the negative of the positive" (SPN, 247). The reference to the entire positive is understood as freedoms that an individual can experience free of constraints by force of government. The repressive and the negative then correspond to the prohibitions that are imposed upon individuals restricting the freedoms that they may choose to experience. The state or government that represents state power of consent, coercion and force (restrictions on freedom), according to Gramsci should be viewed as "punishing bad actions and rewarding praiseworthy and meritorious activity…criminal action or omission must have punitive sanction's" (SPN, 247). By rewards Gramsci is referring to those positive freedoms that are not necessarily codified in law but may be experienced because they are free of restrictions by the state. These are the freedoms that people are allowed experience in their everyday lives without the fear of state punishments (physical force that also can be in the form of fines or other prohibitions on freedoms). How these abstract values are interpreted by the state in the incorporation with the laws that prohibit behaviors, effects the belief systems of individual members of the mass population as to what behaviors within the state are acceptable. It is within these positive freedoms that individual members of the mass population form behaviors that help dictate relationships within collective life. While there is an element of fear of breaking the law that is always present, it is not fear but acts of legal coercion that supports the organized consent[9] or the preferred form of influences over the mass population that makes people chose through their own reasoning to obey the law.

The state by its acts of civilizing, in utilizing this form of coercion, aids in the transformation of individual

---

[9] Outlines of various examples of these legal coercive tools are taken up in the following chapters

members of the mass population into a 'collective individual'. Gramsci uses the term 'collective man' that can be understood as a collective individual. Educative pressures, in part through the courts, is one element that aids in obtaining the mass populations 'consent and their collaboration to the collective life' (SPN, 242). By 'collective life' Gramsci is referring to existing system of relationships within the state that form through joint enterprises in the exercise of these positive freedoms of the mass populations, but here it seems that he is also referring to an acceptance of a general underlining system of beliefs or accepted norms. Most people conform to the law and integrate into subgroups within civil society among those who share common beliefs. The mass population therefore finds a way to experience a way of life collectively in some form social order and this idea of collective life implies that among all subgroups there exist a common set of beliefs that are set as standard by one dominant ideology. So, these common sets of beliefs that are represented in the underlining level of civilizing that is set by the leadership in conjunction with acceptable normative behaviors of positive freedoms that are manifested in civil society create normative behaviors which underscore this collective life. According to Gramsci, "a perfect preparation of the spontaneous consent of the mass who must live those directives, modifying their own habits, their own will, their own convictions to conform to those directives and within the objectives that they propose achieve" (SPN, 266). Pressures are applied by institutions within political society and civil society, together, to coerce the creation of the formation of certain types of relationships within the state. These relationships and how individual members of the mass population act out their positive freedoms are what constitute collective life under an established level of civilizing[10]. The civilizing of the state is the foundation which creates uniformity within the values system that underlines the law but consent to these laws is also dependent on how educative pressures are applied by institutions in civil society. This creation of the level of civilizing by leadership in political society is therefore foundational to supporting how collective life is organized and each of the forces of coercion that exist in superstructure between political and civil society work to offset the other. The collective individual represents any individual member of the mass population who is a willing participant in collective life, and who has conformed their behaviors to the level of civilizing of leadership and the acceptable norms of civil society. As a result of the individual consent to the directives of leadership, the individual then finds a way to exercise their positive freedoms in the pursuit of their own interests. This collective individual then conforms to certain unwritten social sets of social norms created by relationships between other individual members of the mass population. In other words, people in pursuit of their own goals learn or are educated through pressures within the superstructure on how to interact with others and institutions within the state.

Where the state has not imposed restrictions, the mass population is pressured from forces in the superstructure on how positive freedoms are to be experienced. The pressures within the superstructure work to affect how individuals regulate their behaviors among themselves and the institutions within the superstructure and the individual becomes educated in how they experience

---

[10] Pressures that do not include acts of enforcement or physical force upon specific individuals or subgroups.

these positive freedoms. The rewards of the state that Gramsci is describing represent the ability for the mass population to experience a way of life. This represents the freedom of the collective individual to pursue their own interests similarly how Hegel describes how individuals pursue their interests within the state. How the mass population decides to peruse their interests without breaking the law and conforming to social norms can be understood as the "prize winning activities of individuals" once they are educated and consent to leaderships directives (SPN 247). Therefore, the needs of the collective individual can be understood as what freedoms are able to be experienced by the mass population without restriction by the state. These freedoms are in turn influenced by what the mass populations believes that they need to adopt in pursuit of their interests in the state within these confines of the law and a wider system of beliefs within the collective. Ultimately, the collective individual adopts this wider system of beliefs even if they do not understand them yet goes along with the status quo believing that they are better poised in the pursuit of their own interests. This is one of the identifiable breaks from traditional Marxism that Hunt was describing in Gramsci's work. According to Gramsci "because one is acting on essentially on economic forces, reorganizing and developing the apparatus of economic production, creating new structure, the conclusion cannot be drawn that super structural factors should be left to themselves, to develop spontaneously, to the haphazard and sporadic germination" (SPN, 247). Gramsci is pointing out the importance of recognizing the importance that the economy is to the state, what in a large part supports and effects the way of life that can be experienced. This is one essential reason why the individual person chooses to find a way to enter into 'collective life', becoming a

collective individual, in a manner that they believe
supports what they believe are their interests. This
experience of positive freedoms is in a large part
influenced and achievable only through assisting or
contributing to the modes of productive forces. The
economic system of the state affects most relationships
within the state. It is because of the individual belief in
how best to achieve what they believe are their interests,
utilizing their common sense once they consent to
leadership, they find that they need to support their
interests through collaboration with the modes of
productive forces. The state by outlining restricted or
prohibited behaviors limits the freedoms that can be
experienced, affecting the mass populations' view of
what constitutes right and wrong. This in turn affects
their way of thinking, to conform there interests in line
to one dominant ideology. Gramsci says that this
transformation into one dominant ideology does not
have to be entirely complete to have hegemony and
conflicts between the directives of leadership and
ideologies of subgroups within the state are in constant
need of governments intervention to maintain consent.
All freedoms or the entire positive as Gramsci describes,
that the mass population can experience, are not
recognized entirely in laws, such as the ability of
thought; or choices, such as to choose to be a doctor, or
walk up a mountain; people have their own ideologies
but conform to a general dominant one that dictates the
directives of leadership that the mass population
consents to follow. Some of these positive freedoms are
codified into law as positive freedoms or rights such as
those represented in the Canadian *Charter of Rights and Freedoms*.

In Canada, an adopted legal principle is that there is no

crime or punishment without the law – *nullum crimen sine lege, nulla poena lege*, called the legality principle. Gramsci makes reference to the state's "coercive power which legally enforces discipline on those groups who do not consent either actively or passively" (SPN, 12). Force is utilized by the state upon those who do not conform to the directives of leadership. These directives correspond to laws that are intended to maintain or raise the level of civilizing. Courts decide what punishments are appropriate, condemning the prohibited act. As a purely decision-making body or institution, the courts apply the law which initiates state punishments. This force of the state is used at different stages of the court process, but punishments are usually administered once the court has pronounced its judgement only after certain procedures have been utilized to ensure the appearance that a fair determination in a breach of the law occurred. To think of the courts as an enforcement body is not what Gramsci intended. To view the courts as an enforcement body is too great a generalization. It fails to separate the court from other institutions of the state that use physical force against those who do not consent by the law. It fails to identify that the legitimization of the use of force emanates from the coercion of the law and the courts application of the law. State enforcement of the law in the form of punishments serves to reinforce the existing consent of the mass population and therefore maintains organized consent. Gramsci, in discussing the ethical state, finds that that "people are not capable of accepting the law spontaneously, freely, as it is imposed by another class: their must exists an element of coercion or enforcement to the law"(SPN, 263). Here Gramsci identifies two separate forces: one of coercion and the other enforcement, separating the distinction between the two. It is only through coercion or legal coercion that others are influenced into consenting to the law and into accepting the dominant ideology willingly not through fear of punishment.

Gramsci argues that the state in enforcing punishments, should secure the support of public opinion in the manner in which it punishes to maintain organized consent. The state in this way will be better viewed as acting the interests of the mass population when it both punishes crimes that are viewed as immoral and punishes those crimes in a manner that is perceived as morally correct in the eyes of the majority of the mass population. Gramsci finds that consent to the law is achieved when the punishments of the state for transgressions in the law "brings in public opinion as a form of sanction" (SPN, 247). The state should seek the support of public opinion and when public opinion supports the punishment of criminal actions or omissions, then the state is reinforcing the values that are accepted and held by the mass population. These values are proportional to the consent that is given by the mass population to the level of civilizing that is achieved by the state. Public opinion will either condemn or support the enactment or application of a law[11]. Therefore, when punishments are administered by the state, the aim is to have the support of the majority of the mass population so that they agree that the punishment was both legally and morally correct (adherent to some basic principle such as retribution). Public opinion also supports the view in the legitimacy of state action that is crucial in the maintenance of organized consent. If the state has

---

[11] In *An essay on Human Understanding*, Locke emphasizes the importance of public opinion in politics. In comparison to Gramsci, Locke's descriptions of beliefs and the collective are similar to Gramsci and can be found in book four.

obtained the support of public opinion then the state is viewed in the eyes of public opinion as legitimate in its use of force to enforce the law.

Gramsci describes the importance of the perception of the courts as fair to support the maintenance of organized consent. According to Gramsci, when disputes arise, the state through the institution of the court becomes "as guardian of fair play and of the rules of the game" (SPN, 262). Civil law is an area of the law that reconciles rights and liabilities of individual members of the mass population. Gramsci's description of the courts is generalized, and can be applied to different forms of court proceedings. By describing the court as 'guardians of fair play and the guardians of the rules of the game', he is making direct reference to procedural justice. Participants involved in disputes, in courts of all forms of law, are forced to follow procedures that have been designed by the courts and legislatures to give the perception of what constitutes fairness or an appeal to the principle of fairness. In order to obtain active consent to leadership and because the process of conflict resolution is of high importance to the maintenance of organized consent, the court must be perceived as fair so that individual members of the state willfully utilize the courts as an instrument of conflict resolution. For example, in Canada, the establishment that a crime has been committed requires: the act that is prohibited and the required fault element. To establish fault, participants must adherence to a set of legal rules such as evidentiary rules, rules that regulate conduct in court, etc. (both criminal and civil employ different rules to adhere to different types of liability). The rules of fair play in Canada extend to limiting government actions where they themselves must adhere to their own set of procedures that constitute fair play. Fairness in this sense is a principle that the court defines, creating procedural standards of fairness, which they adopt, so at the very least they appear to be operating in a fair and equitable fashion to the matters that are before the court. This perception of fairness contributes to the active consent of the mass population of those who seek redress in the court.

The educative pressure of the courts is one of the most important functions of political society. According to Gramsci, "the school as the positive educative function, and the courts as a repressive and negative educative function, are the most important State activities" (SPN, 258). The educative pressure that is applied by the courts represents the reaffirming of pre-existing organized consent and the values that are projected by leadership to underpin the law. The courts are perceived as protecting the interests of the mass population by their application of the law and the correct application of these principles. The courts apply their educative pressure directly upon those who break the law disciplining and condemning prohibited behaviors. Indirectly the courts decisions reflect upon reinforcement of the convictions of the mass population through forms of media, and written decisions. As an institution of political society, the courts possess their own characteristics and way of modifying the 'cultural environment' through their own educative process. It is common for the general public to be indirectly exposed to the law and the educative pressures of the courts through daily broadcasts in the media, in the form of news and entertainment. Social media plays a significant role in relaying legal opinions and decisions that the courts provide and in providing the general public with an understanding of certain legal concepts, principles and laws. The state according to Gramsci "has consent of the masses and it requests consent at the same time and also educates this consent through by means of the political and syndical associations; these, however, are private organisms, left to the private initiative of the ruling class" (SPN 259). Therefore, in order for the reinforcement of the consent of the mass population to be achieved through the educative pressures of the courts the medias ability to portray the decisions of the courts to the vast population is an important factor in the maintenance of organized consent. The media, such as newspapers, apply their own educative pressure upon collective life or among those that have consented to the level of civilizing of the state, in civil society; activating public opinion and influencing the system of beliefs. Social media places their own twist or opinion on the decisions of leadership that influences the understanding of events. In some instances, the media as they discuss court decisions apply their own understanding of how these decisions will affect collective life and apply educative pressure. While not all of the educative pressures in the super structure are felt exclusively through social media, Gramsci is making reference to how all the different types private institutions within civil society aid in applying their own form of educative pressure on the mass population.

The legal system is at work every day through different means but its effects can sometimes not be felt immediately by everyone. According to Peter McCormick, in his book entitled Canada Courts, the judicial system is

> not something that most people
> personally or directly use every day as

> part of the normal routine of their lives. At and time, only a minority of Canadians will be directly involved in a criminal or civil court action as litigants or witnesses. A few more will take advice from a lawyer on the action or behavior they should follow to accomplish their purposes or the action or behavior they should avoid to stay out of trouble with the law. Most people will do neither. For them, the influence of the courts is more indirect, filtered through the selective, simplified and possibly sensationalized reports in the news media about crimes, arrests, trials, and lawsuits and through the anecdotal penetration of these events into conversations with those around them (McCormack, 13).

Rulings of the court and the enactment of different laws effect the understanding of how the mass population view the way the state functions. The mass population must conform their behaviors to these laws through their understanding of the law provided to them through individuals and institutions within the superstructure. This behavior modification in turn affects how they are able to delegate their own lives within the way of life that is provided by the state and how they can believe that they may achieve their respective goals within the state.

Gramsci's perspective of the law and the courts role in his theory of hegemony is applicable to the examination of different nations states regardless of the state's legal system. In comparison, the Canadian judicial system operates differently than the system in Italy did in Gramsci's time. The Canadian legal system comprises a common law system and a Quebec (the only province to have this French-heritage civil system) juridical legal system. Common law is used in its most general definition here to contrast it against civil law, statue law and delegated legislation. The Italian system at the time of Gramsci was, as it still is today, a strictly civil law system.

> Today, the term common law not only refers to laws set by precedence, but to the system where there are three acknowledged sources of law and where the legislature passes (for example, to codify precedence). This is in contrast to civil law where statutes are more prescriptive and comprehensive. Canada's common-law traditions are why it is not possible to read an act of Parliament or a regulation or order and expect to have a full understanding of its application and implications. We will see that even the Constitution is subject to the interpretation by the judiciary. (Harder, 5)

The act of interpretation allows the Courts to apply their own opinions into the interpretation of the law, creating common law. The Italian legal system of the 1900's placed judges in a less active role restrained from adding their own opinions to the law.

> Always acknowledged as a pivotal factor of differentiation between

> common law systems and civil law
> systems, this peculiar style of legal
> thinking has been labeled as 'systematic
> conceptualism', as opposed to an
> "inductive problem-solving approach"
> that would constitute the heart of legal
> reasoning at common Law.
> Nevertheless, the supposed unbridgeable
> opposition must be mitigated and the
> description of the perspective of the
> Italian legal system to the problem of
> qualification might be useful in
> signaling not too slender commonalities
> between common law and civil law
> mode of thought in legal matters.
> (Bashiera, 286).

Under the Italian civil law system (also known as code law), as it was in Gramsci's trial, judge's rulings are primarily based on adhering to the letter of the law or what is 'encoded' in the statue. Gramsci seemed to have ignored the significance of this characteristic of the common law courts in his references to the courts educative role. Common law jurisdictions gave judges more power to influence outcomes at trials by providing their own opinion and interpretation of the law according to the factual evidence which makes them identifiable as an institution of ideological production.

Recently, in Italy there has been a movement towards de-codification; "a pivotal re-adjustment in the shape of the role played by judges, who became increasingly influential in law making, has taken place in the Italian legal system" (Bashiera, 289). This movement reflects the need for judges to be more influential in comparison to their counterparts in common law jurisdictions where judges play more of a role in creating laws that arise out of their powers of interpretation and ability to apply the law in given circumstances that are before them. In Canada, judges create new law from their ability to interpret statues and apply reasoning to discern the intention of those that drafted statues. In other words, the courts can interpret what the purposes behind the enactment of a statue was at the time of its drafting by legislatures. This power of interpretation and judicial pronouncements or judge-made law, is a characteristic which allows the courts in common law systems to be an institution that produces the means of ideological production in the state. This is something that Gramsci would not have readily observed given the perspective of the Italian civil legal system. In common law jurisdictions, judges can draw upon a multitude of ideological resources, that include councils' legal briefs, to justify their reasoning of their decisions. Lawyers in offering advice to clients then convey this same ideology to the general public that serves to further the effects of the educative role of the courts by reaffirming existing law. Lawyers also aid in appealing to the conception drawn by the courts and legislatures on the interpretation of legal principles or values that are prescribed in the law. The active participation in the court system by governments and subgroups serves to aid in the maintenance of organized consent. According to Gramsci the inability of the Italian bourgeoisie to unite the people around them was "the cause of its defeats and the interruptions in its developments (SPN, 53). The courts must be viewed as fair and impartial so that they appeal to the general public as an institution that is legitimate in not only administering punishments but in acting as a referee in mitigating disputes. This process of initiating court proceedings is an important part of civilizing within the state. Gramsci places a high degree of importance for leadership to gain and then maintain organized consent if it is to continue to successfully lead.

Chapter three:
The Canadian court system

In Canada, there are different jurisdictional courts. Each court hears different types of legal disputes, such as criminal or civil matters. The courts are also arranged in a hierarchal order involving avenues of appeals to higher courts that provide the ability to dispute findings of lower courts on facts of law. The appeals process is important in itself to further the development of the law that will meet the needs of an evolving state. At the top of this ordering of courts sits the Supreme Court of Canada that presides over all of these different courts and acts as the final court of appeal of Canada.

> The judiciary is broken into a system of courts with parallel systems with federal, provincial, and military jurisdictions. Above each of these is a court of appeals, and superior to each of these (since 1873) is the Supreme Court of Canada. A court has limited authority to make incremental changes to the law (i.e., new president) for subordinate courts. Ultimately, the Supreme Court of Canada may set president for all other courts in the country. In addition to following precedent set by superior Canadian courts, lower courts must also consider decisions of their equals and should not stray dramatically from them, though they are not strictly bound to follow such decisions. (Harder, 8)

The Supreme Court of Canada creates uniformity in the law throughout Canada making sure that the laws in Canada all apply to the constitution and various rulings in common law, through the process of litigation. While

Canada is under legislative supremacy it is the Supreme Court of Canada is the governments body ultimately tasked as referee when conflicts arise between acts of legislatures and the interests of the subordinate groups. The Supreme Courts educative pressure is limited to matters that come before it.

The Canadian system of governance is a form of legislative supremacy. The political structure of Canada comprises three parts of governance the executive, legislature and the judiciary. These three branches of government comprise the political structure of Canada where the control of the coercive apparatus of the state presides. According to Gramsci, the state is identified as a relationship of forces.

> Unity of the State in the differentiation of powers: Parliament more closely linked to civil society; the judiciary power, between government and Parliament, represents the continuity of the written law (even against the government). Naturally all three powers are also organs of political hegemony, but in different degrees 1. Legislature; 2 Judiciary; 3 Executive. It is to be noted how lapses in administration of justice make an especially disastrous impression on the public: the hegemonic apparatus is more sensitive in this sector (SPN, 246).

The public or all of the members of mass population is more sensitive in how they mold their opinions of government by how justice is administered in the state, according to Gramsci more than any other branch. The judicial branch consists of a variety of independent courts including the final court of appeal for Canada, the Supreme Court of Canada.

The Canadian system comprises three levels of government. These levels comprise the federal provincial and municipal levels. According to Ian Greene in his book entitled *The Charter of Rights*,

> legislative supremacy may seem like a straightforward legal concept that has no obvious connection with civil liberties. After the Glorious Revolution of 1688, it was accepted that the legislative branch of government could determine the powers of the other two branches: the executive (which became known as the cabinet and the public service) and the judiciary. Canada inherited the principle of legislative supremacy pursuant to the preamble of the BNA Act, which stated that Canada would have a constitution "similar in principle to that of the United Kingdom (Greene 15).

Legislative supremacy, a concept of constitutional law that means that the legislature is supreme over the other two branches of government. In other words, the executive and judicial branches are subordinate to the legislative branch but much controversy surrounds such labeling because of the power that the Supreme Court has to strike down legislation if they find that it is in contravention of the Constitution Act of 1982 or the Charter of Rights and Freedoms. The legislative body is generally considered to be the decision makers who prescribe policy for Canada that is consistent with certain values and a system of beliefs that are said to be representative of democracy in Canada and representative of the Canadian system of governance[12].

The members of the Canadian Parliament and the nine Judges of the Supreme Court of Canada would be viewed by Gramsci as 'functionary intellectuals'. The purpose of 'functionary intellectuals' is to promote the ideology of the dominant social group. According to Gramsci, these "intellectuals are the dominants group's 'deputies' exercising the subaltern function of social hegemony and political government" (SPN, 12). These intellectuals promote the dominant ideology in the performance of the job which supports maintenance of organized consent. According to Roger S. Gottlieb, in his book entitled *An Anthology of Western Marxism*, the

> *elite* amongst them must have the capacity to be an organizer of society in general, including all its complex organism of services, right up to the state organism, because of the need to create the conditions most favorable to the expansion of their own class; or at the least they must possess the capacity to choose the deputies (specialized employees) to whom to entrust this

---

[12] The executive branch has the power to enact laws but its limited.

> activity of organizing the general system of relationships external to the business itself. It can be observed that the "organic" intellectuals which every new class creates alongside itself and elaborates in the course of its development, are for the most part "specializations" of partial aspects of the primitive activity of the new social type which the new class has brought into prominence (Gottlieb, 113).

Judges and politicians are examples of 'functionary' intellectuals. The relationship between how their role in political society and how they further the maintenance of organized consent exists in their 'functionary' roles. Each are responsible for the "[organization of] the hegemony of the dominant social group" (SPN,12). The Supreme Court of Canada as the final court of appeal for Canada creates uniformity in the law according to the underlining values of civilizing. By interpreting and applying Statue, the Courts create finality to controversial issues that arise out of conflicts (these conflicts are by the very nature of the Court are to involve legal issues). Often the courts and the Supreme Court is no different become the institution where subgroups appeal to the values under the law to seek change or redress from interventions that they believe are actions of government that are arguably infringing on these values.

The Supreme Court of Canada is not easily accessible by those subgroups which may seek redress in this manner. Assuming, that the Court would even agree to hear a case or matter, there is a high financial cost to those who would seek legal redress through this avenue. One characteristic of the court system in Canada is that the more monetary means that is available to the person or subgroup, normally means better access to the judicial system in comparison to others with less financial means. These conditions of class have been created in part by lawyers[13], charging high prices for their services, creating a condition that makes it difficult for the average individual in society to access to the court. For example, to access the Supreme Court of Canada, that can often involve a lengthy process where the average individual would find the costs involved astronomical[14] (cost mainly depends on the average price that council will charge a client for representation although considerations to the contrary may involve council that could represent client's pro bono but this is not the norm). This restrictive access to the final Court of Appeal contributes to the passive consent by those who would rather leave the decisions to those in political and judicial power to make decisions. Passively they refrain from actively questioning leadership and challenging government decisions through court proceedings despite whether they find any of their actions questionable. Considerations as to the weight of other tribunal courts and low courts but in general any court action that involves the need for council is costly. Appeal courts whereby there is an automatic right to appeal from lower court decisions only incur additional costs form what clients have already spent at the lower court or tribunal level.

---

[13] Accessing the legal system in Canada can be an expensive venture considering the costs of council and as in most civil cases risky depending on the amounts of monies that are at stake to a party involved. In this sense, it is unfair.

[14] Through the process of reference, subgroups within society can actively participate in the process as intervenors.

Chapter four:
Reference question an instrument of legal coercion

There are various instruments of legal coercion created and utilized by the state to support the maintenance of organized consent. According to Gramsci legislatures "formulate directives which will become a norm of conduct for the others, but at the same time creates instruments by means which the directives themselves will be imposed, and by means of which it will verify their execution" (SPN, 266). These instruments, such as the creation of certain legal procedures, conventions, support for private institutions, support resolving disputes in a manner that allows the state to gain organize consent out of conflict or potential conflicts. Gramsci identifies that "elected career officials... [as having] at their disposal the legal coercive powers of the state" (SPN, 266). These instruments are themselves protected under the law and enforced by the state. Gramsci describes the law as naturally coercive because it is imposed upon the mass population by another class (SPN, 263). The law in general despite what may seem to be a sensible rule is coercive according to Gramsci simple because it is imposed. Legislatures while they create laws (courts in common law jurisdictions also create laws) they also create legal instruments of coercion or the legal ways of imposing their directives. One example of a coercive instrument legally created in Canada, that is worth examining to illustrate Gramsci's point, is the process of governments posing reference questions to the Court.

The Supreme Court of Canada provides opinions on questions that are referred to it on reference to assist

Parliament in their decision-making. This process of reference allows Parliament to formally ask the Supreme Court of Canada direct questions. Although these questions are political in nature, they normally involve some aspect of constitutional law. According to Kate Puddster, in her paper *Unraveling Reference Questions: Theoretical and Political Implications in a Canadian Context,*

> through section 53 of the Supreme Court Act (RSC 1985, c S-26) or various provisions created by provincial legislatures, the executive branch (more specifically, the Governor in-Council or the Lieutenant Governor-in-Council) can pose questions directly in front of the Supreme Court (or provincial courts of appeal). The reference power provides governments the ability to completely sidestep the normal litigation routes, resulting in a privileged access to the courts for the executive that is denied to citizens, interest groups, legislatures, or opposing political parties (Puddster, 1).

Court procedures are designed to protect the interests of parties involved thereby promoting a concept of fairness or fair play. According to the Supreme Court in *Reference Governor-General in Council* [1910] 43 SCC 536; fairness was the consideration in the process of the system of appeals, to create uniformity in the law.

Only Parliament has this direct access to the Supreme Court of Canada to ask advisory opinions. The provinces have to refer their questions to their respective provincial court of appeals and then they can have a subsequent appeal to the Supreme Court of Canada.

> the reference question procedure, allows the executive (of both the federal and provincial governments) to obtain an advisory judicial opinion from a Court of Appeal or the Supreme Court of Canada on the constitutionality of government legislation, either proposed or enacted, in the absence of a live legal dispute (Puddster, 1).

It gives Parliament priority to utilize the vast expertise of the nine members of the Court, to advise them on particular issues of concern. Provinces are not excluded from utilizing the reference procedure but it is through an indirect channel. They first must refer their questions to their respective provincial courts of appeal first before they can further their matter to the Supreme Court of Canada. The idea is that once decisions are rendered in their respective provincial appellate courts, only then can the provinces further an appeal to the Supreme Court of Canada. The Court will then look at the question or questions posed to it and render its opinion with written reasons outlining their decision. In instances the Court will reserve to not render an opinion.

An advisory opinion on a question of reference does not create any formal obligation upon governments to follow the advice of the Court. According to Gerald Rubin in his paper, *The Nature, Use and Effect of Reference Cases in Canadian Constitutional Law*,

> the advisory opinion binds no one, not even the judges, it is not rendered between parties, it is given to the asking official or department and is often rendered without hearing argument. In all these respects, it differs from the declaratory judgment. Even if argument is heard by parties with opposing interests . . . it lacks one of the essential elements of a judgment in that it is rendered not on demand of and to an aggrieved or complaining party, but on demand of and to an administrative body (Rubin, 1).

The main aspect of the reference questions is that they do not develop through lower court decisions but derive their substance from political debate. As a result, the answers provided by the Court are potentially politically charged. Therefore, the Courts answers will influence the political outcomes often enough regardless of how the Court may consider how to answer the questions posed to it. Unlike most court proceedings the Court does not have the traditional luxury of hearing arguments that have been developed from the lower courts and they do not have a benefit of reviewing the decisions of lower court judge where a live feature of litigants exists.

Inherited from England, the reference question process has existed in Canada as long as the Supreme Court of Canada has existed. This advisory model of England is outlined in the *Judicial Committee Act* of 1833 (Rand,

15). The Act stated that under section 4, "the executive may refer any such matters whatsoever as His Majesty shall think fit to the Court expecting them to render their opinion" (Judicial Committee Act, 1833). The Judicial Committee of the Privy Council or JCPC was the final court of Appeal for Canada who heard the majority of Canada's reference cases. Since 1948 the Supreme Court of Canada has been the final Court of Appeal in Canada when the JCPC no longer acted as the final court of appeal for Canada. During the time leading up to 1948, the executive and Parliament, in both Canada and England (and other commonwealth countries), had almost limitless power to refer anything in the form of a question to the JCPC. These questions were a) important enough to the English Parliament that they needed help in answering them and b) consisted of questions concerning the law alone (Rand, 10).

Initially, reference questions had a key role to play in relation to the Parliamentary power of disallowance. Constitutional law in part deals with the allocation of powers. Once these powers are allocated then administrative law involves how these various institutions in political society exercise these powers. Parliament under their power of disallowance could arbitrarily override powers of the provinces in the creation of legislation if it chose to do so. As a result of this treatment, the provinces slowly began enacting their own legislation that allowed them to refer questions to the Supreme Court of Canada (Rubin, 1). The conflict often arose if Parliament claimed power over certain areas that the provinces clearly thought they had power over. These claims meant that this left less money for the provinces in terms of government funding,

> the strongest moving force for use of the reference power is a desire by both the federal (and provincial) executive for a 'speedy judicial determination of legal problems arising out of the interpretation of the provisions of the British North America Act and especially the provisions allotting legislative jurisdiction (Rubin, 170).

As prescribed under sections 91 and 92 of the BNA Act respectively, Parliament, and often the provinces, needed to resolve issues of constitutionality arising mainly out of questions of the division of powers. These antagonisms between the provinces and the federal Parliament in Canada might be representative of what Gramsci calls an 'unstable equilibrium between classes' (SPN, 245). As Canada began to break away from the control of England some classes might have been unhappy with the transition that Canada was going under as one group namely England's domination was losing its dominance to a ruling class in Canada. According to Gramsci, this type of unstable equilibrium between classes "is the result of the fact that certain categories of intellectuals (in direct service of the state, especially civil and military bureaucracy) are still too closely tied to the old dominant classes" (SPN, 245). This is taken out of the context that Gramsci is applying this quotation. He is using an illustration to expand on his concept of regime change from a period in Italy when the church had a large amount of influence in the old regime in comparison to the new regime where the church had little political influence. But, this is an example that Gramsci uses to pull out the idea that there are conflicts in classes as an old regime replaces the new. To try and draw a potential comparison to Gramsci's point, in Canadian history; it was not the church but the monarchy of England and there may be evidence of intellectuals within the provinces that challenged Parliament or Federal power through reference questions to the Court that were resistant to this change into a Canada that was severing its ties and while a more centralized form of Canadian governance formed challenging the powers of the province traditionally maintained.

Between the late 1800's to early 1900's, the Canadian government was slowly gaining its independence from England. As a result, fewer Canadian reference cases were being heard by the JCPC. As this power of Canada's final Court of Appeal was transferring over to the Supreme Court of Canada it was not initially mirroring the JCPC's decision making process on questions posed on reference. In the *McCarthy reference case* [1890] SCC, the Supreme Court of Canada's decision proved "problematic for the very reason that they ruled against Parliament without providing a reason for their decision" (Mathen, 4)

> This was one of the principle reasons behind the introduction in the House of

> Commons of the Hon. Edward Blake's
> resolution of 1890 on references which
> in turn led to the amendment in 1891 of
> the reference pro visions of the Supreme
> Court Act (Rubin, 170).

This amendment made it mandatory for the Court to render more than a 'yes' or 'no' answer to a question posed to it. The argument is that if the Court's decisions are not articulated in the form of written reasoning then Parliament cannot gain anything from referring questions to the Court. The Court's reluctance to provide clearly articulated reasons made the Courts involvement in political issues affairs less likely. For this reason, the Court may have been reluctant to provide outlined reasoning, fearing that their decision was too politically charged. The degree that the Court would influence politics depends on two things: how the Court chooses to answer questions and how these questions were framed by government. The problem with questions that are posed to the Court on reference is that they may be framed in such a way that beg political answers and the Courts early conduct seemed wary of influencing politics.

The Court was intended to provide guidance through the written articulation of their decisions on reference questions. In this light, in 1891 the Act was re-appealed "to clarify that the Supreme Court must respond to matters of reference. This role is echoed today under section 53 of the Supreme Court act" (Mathen, 4). In an opinion rendered in the decision of *References by the Governor-General in Council* [1910] 43 SCC 536:

> We must not forget that judges are

> officers of the Crown, and I adopt without any reserve the opinion expressed by Dorion C J., a man of wide political and judicial experience, when, speaking for the full Court of the Queen's Bench in Quebec, he said in Bruneau et al v Massue: The Judges of the Superior Court as citizens are bound to perform all the duties which are imposed upon them by either the Dominion or the local Legislature ("Government of Canada", 2017).

This was a very profound statement, that every court in Canada does not work for itself but works in joint with the rest of the government institutions. No different, the Supreme Court of Canada in its performance in reference cases must be in compliance with the proper administration of the Canadian government. On matters referred to the Court there is no written rule that says that the federal government has to follow the Courts (Huscroft, 16). To some degree the Court were aware that answering politically charged questions would influence politics. The Supreme Court, pre-Charter, was very cautious not to step too far over this line. Arguably, it would be improper for the Supreme Court to choose what questions on reference it would or would not answer. There exists a co-operative aspect to government between the interaction of its institutions. This was well established in 1891 by re-appealing this Act, bringing the role of the Supreme Court as a help mate to matters important to the Legislative body of Canada.

The only legislation which framed the reference procedure in Canada was under the *Supreme Court Act* (R.S.C. 1985, c. S-26). Created in 1875, the *Supreme Court Act* (R.S.C. 1985, c. S-26), prescribes Parliaments right to pose questions of reference. With some significant amendments from its beginnings, section 53 of the *Supreme Court Act* (R.S.C. 1985, c. S-26), grants Parliament the power to pose questions on reference to the Supreme Court (Huscroft, 4). New amendments to Section 53 began a new dawn of how references were going to be handled:

> Section 53(1) specifies a requirement of important questions of law or fact that concern essentially matters of constitutionality, subsection (2) immediately renders this limitation redundant by extending the reference power to questions of law or fact concerning any matter the government sees fit to submit. For greater certainty, subsection (2) precludes the Court from limiting any matter by means *of esjudem generis* interpretation. Subsection (3) precludes the Court from using the important question modifier to limit the reference power by deeming any question referred by the government an important question (Huscroft, 4)

This sounds ominously similar to what was spelled out in *the Judicial Committee Act* 1833; giving the Parliament the power to ask any question it wanted to the Court. The power of Parliament under section 53, seems 'limitless' as to what they may ask in terms of questions to the Supreme Court (Huscroft, 4). But what had happened as a result of the new amendment to section 53 the Court began interpreting how and what questions it would answer. It was not until the *Charter of rights and Freedoms* that the new role of the Court became transparent.

The evolution of the Court in the early 1980's transformed how references cases were to be decided. Just shortly before the Charter was patriated it seemed as if the Courts were preparing for their more active role that they would take in answering reference questions. According to Michael Mandel in his book entitled, *The Charter of Rights and the Legalization of politics in Canada*,

> in 1980 the Supreme Court made the extraordinarily unjudicial pronouncement that everything it said in a case, whether necessary to the decision or not, was binding on lower courts, thus abandoning the most fundamental limiting rule of judicial authority, a defining feature of stare dicisis itself, the hallowed distinction between, ratio decendi and obiter dicta (M. Mandel 29).

What changed was that reference cases were now framed to be alike all other judicial decisions, although they were still characterized as Court opinions.

> by 1981 the advisory opinion was firmly entrenched in Canada, and occupied a significant portion of the Court's docket.

> Early changes to the Supreme Court Act ensured that references would take the same form as cases. Certain parties enjoyed statutory rights of participation, and others could be granted standing, evidence could be received, pleadings prepared, *amici* appointed and reasons would always be forthcoming (Mathen, 151).

With the changes in *Supreme Court Act* and subsequent Court rulings, the landscape of all reference cases changed forever. However slowly, the Court has developed this power through careful evaluation of its past roles as advisor to Parliament. This advisory role of the court was intended to ensure that the newly elected governments were complying with ideological values that have been in place before the new leadership came into power. Reference questions help to ensure that the dominant ideology continues and build to meeting various needs of the state.

The *Patriation reference case* of [1981] 1 SCC 753, marked a new era in reference cases and judicial activism. The Court in this reference case was asked various questions pertaining to whether or not the federal government could patriate the Canadian constitution and how it could go about it. The very nature of one of the questions posed was a question on a convention. This question in particular was in regards to what constituted enough support of the provinces (how many provinces were needed to support the action of Parliament) for Trudeau's government to go ahead and patriate the

Constitution Act of 1982. The question raised was whether they need all, none or some of the provinces support. According to Peter Russell, in his paper, *The Patriation and Quebec Veto References: The Supreme Court Wrestles with the Political Part of the Constitution*,

> [since] there was no written constitutional text on the requirements for a Canadian request to the U.K. Parliament to amend Canada's Constitution, if the Court agreed to answer the questions posed in the reference, it could not avoid dealing with arguments based on unwritten constitutional convention (Russel, 70).

This case defines the beginning of judicial activism and the Charter. The major defining aspect of this case is that the Court was asked to give their opinion on a matter of convention. The question posed according to M Mandel:

> Is it consistent with constitutional convention (understood as meaning, roughly, a historically recognized norm of political behavior) for the federal government to approach the UK Parliament over such substantial opposition (M. Mandel, 24)?

This type of question had nothing to do with written law and there was no precedent for the Courts to follow. "When the courts were asked to answer on constitutional convention they were asked something outside the realm of law and judging" (Mandel, 28). What makes this so unusual is that the Court found it necessary to answer.

The *Patriation reference case* of [1981] 1 SCC 753, was a very politically charged issue. Parliament was fishing for an answer that they could interpret as allowing them to go forward with a limited amount of support of the provinces to patriate the Charter. As a result, they chose very vague questions to pose to the Court (M. Mandel, 34). But the Court's decision was broad enough on the issue of their answer on convention that both the federal government and the provinces were interpreting the decision differently. The Courts ruling in the *Patriation reference case* [1981] 1 SCC 753, was interpreted differently by governments on different sides of the argument. According to M. Mandel, "it was interpreted differently according to which side of the issue and which side of the Quebec border one was on" (M. Mandel 29). This is both an example of the importance of the Court outlining precisely their reasoning of the Court and when the Court should not answer issues that are not on a solid legal ground. The problem is that sometimes customs of government like conventions decide, as they did in this case, how proper constitutional law is to be administered or handled. The Supreme Courts seemingly knew this, which was the reason why the Supreme Court chose to answer the question on convention, aiding in settling such an important issue that the country was facing. Alternatively, questions surround the fact that Trudeau packed

the Supreme Court with his appointees and as
such may have expected a favorable answer that
would serve his interests.

Part of this new evolution of the Charter era, the Court
began to map out on its own, clearly defined parameters
of how it would rule in reference cases. This
transformation deviated from the old role that it played
in its inability to refuse to answer questions posed to it
pre- Charter. These parameters were clearly outlined in
the *Succession Reference case* [1998] 2 SCC 217, where
the Court held that:

> since reference questions may clearly be
> interpreted as directed to legal issues,
> the Court is in a position to answer
> them. The Court cannot exercise its
> discretion to refuse to answer questions
> on a pragmatic basis. These questions
> raise issues of fundamental public
> importance and they are not too
> imprecise or ambiguous to permit a
> proper legal answer. Nor has the Court
> been provided with insufficient
> information regarding the present
> context in which the questions arise.
> Finally, the Court may deal with
> reference issues that might otherwise be
> considered not yet ripe for decision
> (*Succession reference Quebec*, [1998] 2
> SCC 217).

The Court is now defining when it will refuse to answer
questions without the need of prescribed legislation.
This may be a result of accusations of the public that the

Court was too politically active in the *Patriation reference case* [1981]. If the Court had refused to answer the particularly politically charge question on reference how different would the outcome of the charter have been?

This case provides a clear example of how the Courts were given more power under the Charter to be more judicially active. In the *Succession reference case* [1998] 2 SCC 217, the issue was a very politically sensitive issue on Quebec's right to separate from Canada. With the population in Quebec already highly sensitive to the issue, as was the rest of Canada, the Court

> decided to rely on basic and abstract principles that were not explicitly written out in the constitution, but were major elements of the architecture of the Constitution itself (Charter) and are as such its lifeblood (Roach, 129).

The Court found that unilateral succession by Quebec would be unconstitutional; the message that was sent to Parliament was one that they should negotiate the separation of Quebec, if by majority vote they wanted to separate (Roach, 129). The decision was notably giving Parliament direction, but the Supreme Court could have arguable just said that there was no provision in constitutional law that would grant Quebec any such right. The fact was that the Court went further in their interpretive power by pushing what can be interpreted by the wording of the Charter (Roach, 139). This reference case illustrates how the Supreme Court were pushing the boundaries of their judicial role by providing their own interpretation of already vague descriptions of rights or ambiguity contained the Charter at and from what they thought to be the intensions of its framers. They are no longer interpreting law but interpreting the intentions of people who drafted the legislature or close to guessing the intentions of the framers. This new role of the Court seems to be the equivalent of pulling rabbits out of thin air. In other words, they seem to have been making interpretations without reliance to any concrete evidence of fact.

There is an illusion that has been projected since the inception of the Charter that the Courts are able to dictate politics. Judges can be no more politically correct over politically charged issues than the politicians that pose reference questions in the first place. According to Radakrishnan Persaud, in his dissertation entitled *THE ROLE OF JUDICIAL ADVISORY OPINIONS IN CANADIAN CONSTITUTIONALISM AND FEDERALISM: THE SENATE, PATRIATION & QUEBEC VETO REFERENCE CASES CONSIDERED* "there is the erroneous assumption that correct legal answers to reference questions exist, and that the Judges are likely to decide according to those correct answers" (Persaud, 2). The government has a wide range of legal scholars at their disposal excluding the Court Judges who are a phone call away. It seems as if the government themselves is taking chances that the Court will decide the correct way. If the government has a good grasp of the situation at hand then a ruling by the Court would only give some finality to a given situation. However, the Court by determining an answer it serves to remove government from any blame. Therefore, government can defuse any politically sensitive issue by referring questions to the Courts. The Judges are in no fear of reprisals because they are not elected but appointed figures.

The *Marriage reference* [2004] 3 SCC 698, represents a Parliamentary decision to refer a politically charged issue at the Courts. It is also an example of how the Courts contribute to the government's ability to raise level of civility in state. At the time of this ruling traditional subgroups within civil society representing constituents who were opposed to this proposed legislation by Parliament. This left the issue as a potential hotbed of political controversy from these various groups that included various church organizations. Parliament referred four separate questions on the matter to the Supreme Court of Canada.

> In fact, the government could have introduced legislation establishing same-sex marriage into Parliament at any time. It chose to invoke the reference procedure, however, because it was keen to diffuse its responsibility for establishing same-sex marriage. It knew that the introduction of legislation following the receipt of favorable answers on the reference questions would help neutralize political opposition, and as far as the government was concerned, the longer the Court took in dealing with the reference the better (Huscroft, 8).

While, this is one interpretation of Parliaments motive, it seems reasonable that there was no real legal question to answer and that Parliament was reluctant to initiate same-sex marriage into law by itself. Citizen participation in theory represents what is thought to be foundational to the Canadian conception of democracy. This case is an example of active citizen participation in government through court action, represented by a subgroup within society who sought to deal with an inequality and injustice pervading their daily lives through the judicial system that they believed was a social imperative. Just as in the *Patriation reference* 1981 and the *Succession reference* 1998, this case is another example of how the Courts were turned into a mechanism for the advancement of politics. By playing politics in this manner the Court is effectively involved in raising the level of civility in the state to a large extent than ever before. This was not a case of fact finding, but one where politicians needed to defuse any potential back lash from their constituents on such a controversial issue or at least the motive seemed to be purely political. Leadership maintains organized consent in this manner by deflecting or passing controversial issues to the Court to decide. Considering, the potential moral implications that were involved in the question, why then would it seem that the Court was better equipped to decide? In the interests of gaining the popular vote politicians divert attention away from them by refereeing contentious issues to the Court to answer.

What is unique in this case is that the Court refused to answer the fourth question that was posed to it. The fourth question posed to the Court was arguably the most important question out of all of them. The question asked:

> Is the opposite-sex requirement for marriage for civil purposes, as

> established by the common law and set
> out for Quebec in section 5 of the
> Federal Law–Civil Law Harmonization
> Act, No. 1, consistent with the Canadian
> Charter of Rights and Freedoms? If not,
> in what particular or particulars and to
> what extent (Huscroft, 9)?

It seems fair that Parliament asked this question, whether the term equality as defined under the Charter encompassed its proposed legislation. In short, the Court has made clear on several occasions that it will not answer reference questions that it does not want to answer. There is only one problem with this: "[t]he Court has never established that it has the power to refuse to answer reference questions" (Huscroft, 9). By refusing to answer the Court was clearly sending the message that not only should Parliament work it out but sent a similar message that the issue was not important enough for the Court to consider. "The Court thought it was more important to stay out of the same-sex marriage issue than to resolve any lingering constitutional uncertainty about it" (Huscroft, 10). Another problem with the Courts exercising its obligation to refuse to answer encapsulates the same problem that it is saying it's trying to deter. The Courts are becoming more politically active because they are determining which political issue is more or less worthy of being answered. By picking and choosing they determine how they affect politics. The issue for the Court in refusing to answer was not bound up with the moral decision itself but it saw from the onset that there was no legal basis to some of the questions that it was asked to answer.

At the foundation of animosity directed at the reference

procedure from legal scholars on the Courts role since the Charter, is this re-occurring theme of judicial activism. This accusation of judicial activism casts the Courts in a bad light but it sheds light on how organized consent is maintained by the Court. The argument is that the Court should not be used to address, decide or render an opinion on issues that are best left up to politicians to decide. Since the Charter the Supreme Court has been its most judicially active. One problem is that, "governments have infrequently sought references as a way of defusing political or legal crises; viz" (Dodek, 121). It is in this sense that the lines between politics and law have become blurry when politicians abuse this power beginning with the use of reference questions that began Pre-Charter. With a lack of development from lower court rulings the Supreme Court is thrown into an arena of politics and law. "Political actors involved in these highly contentious political episodes abide by the decisions made by the courts in reference cases, making these decisions more binding than advisory in nature" (Puddster, 2). The Court is thrust into the role of political referee by initiating the reference process and then with the advent of the Charter they were more inclined to settle political disputes by appealing to Charter values. Some of these Charter values represent various codified rights in the Charter while others represent interpretations of the rights. It is the Courts themselves who often decide how these values are applied in various cases. According to Mandel "[the] Charter, "in its substitution of judicial representative forms and of abstract/principle for concrete/policy forms of argument for the resolution of political controversy, represents a fundamental change in the structure of Canadian political life, a legalization of politics" (Mandel, 81-82). The Courts have become more active since the Charter's Patriation but from this point, arguments among legal scholars differ whether it was the Charter itself that has caused the issue of placing judicial activism in a bad light or it was that the courts who decided to take judicial activism themselves. Under the Charter, the ideological premise of the Trudeau government was that the Courts would be entrusted with the securing of the rights of the people against the intrusive tendencies of the government. The problem is not the Charter but how it has been used.

In contrast, the stance taken by Kent Roach is that the Charter promotes a dialogue between Parliament and the Courts. This means that the judicial activism that others criticize the courts for, is actually representative of proper dialogue between these two branches of government. In other words, the Judges are not dictating politics and acting on their own. He argues that what is being defined by some as judicial activism, is actually not an expression of the Courts stepping into the political arena. According to Roach "the Canadian debate about judicial activism reflects original hostility to the enactment of the Charter by some conservative Tories and democratic socialists" (Roach, 291). He argues that while the Courts can place checks and balances on Parliament, it is Parliament that has the power to override those powers under sections 1 and 33 of the Charter (Roach, 7). As a result of this ability, he argues that, "the Canadian Charter does not give fallible and unelected Judges the last word over matters that involve rights and freedoms (Roach, 7). Section 1 allows the Parliament and provinces to limit certain rights as they are expressed under the Charter given proper justification (Roach, 4). This limit can be found to be unconstitutional by an appeal to the Court and if the Court finds that the government acted unfairly. But more strongly worded is section 33 "provides [Parliament] or provincial legislature may expressly declare that any law shall operate notwithstanding a provision" (M. Mandel, 87). Therefore "all that governments need to do is to take responsibility for enacting ordinary legislation that justifiably limits or clearly overrides rights as interpreted by the Court (Roach, 7). The idea that Roach is expressing is that there is an expressed dialogue that goes on between the Courts and legislatures where one respects the other, knowingly that both can threaten to ignore either if necessary. This argument, while valid in theory does not seem to be at all practical in its application. While the drafters of the Charter may have implied that the Courts and governments work together, this dialogue was already substantiated in matters of reference from the time of the JCPC. Reference questions were intended to establish a cooperation between Parliament and the Courts, before the provinces began their own reference campaign and before the Charter itself. Part of the controversy is that there exist formal amendment procedures to change the constitution and Parliaments just seems to let the courts determine constitutional meanings without having to amend constitutional law. So, what rule allows the courts to do this? None, it just seems to be allowed because of the ambiguity inherent in the language of the Charter where Judges broaden or lessen the meaning of some right and freedoms.

The stronger argument is that the responsibility for influencing the political outcomes that result from the use of reference questions since the advent of the Charter solely rests on the Court. This implies that the unelected officials of the Court have a role in creating a balancing effect in the relationship between interests in the state or what Gramsci calls 'organic continuity' that helps maintain organized consent[15]. Parliament will not just choose to ignore the Court and not follow their answers to the questions posed to them on reference. In this light, Parliament must act upon decisions rendered on reference:

> the rejection of the Courts opinion in reference cases would be futile even if it was somehow a viable political option: inevitably, action taken contrary to the Court's opinion would lead to litigation and, barring a significant change in circumstances, the Court could be reaffirmed the opinion it provided in the reference case. As a practical matter, it would be under enormous pressure to do so, for its credibility and institutional authority would be at stake (Huscroft, 2).

The Courts actions are therefore a binding force in reference cases in all respects of stare dicisis (precedent setting). Therefore, the Court themselves has changed their role back into an enforcement role in matters referred to them on reference. But the non-enforceable role was only in spirt and not a practical description because opinions of the Court were always enforceable. Their opinions however abstract have always been influential and binding. If an opinion was ever challenged (if that was possible because how could an opinion be challenged in the first place) how could the

---

[15] See, Chapter five for Gramsci's use of organic continuity (p 27).

challenge ever be successful if the highest Court in the land, in theory, had already made an opinion on the matter. In practice Parliament will not just choose to ignore the decision of the Courts because it would be undermining the very foundation of the Court if it did. So, when Parliament poses an abstract question asking for an interpretation of abstract values the Courts are now presiding over politics.

Chapter five:
Raising the level of civilizing in the interests of the ruling class

The state tries to avoid the perception of being bureaucratized in how it civilizes. According to Gramsci this act of civilizing by the state represents a "danger of becoming democratized, it is true; but every organic continuity presents this danger, which must be watched. The danger of discontinuity, of improvisation is still greater" (SPN, 196). This reaffirms why Gramsci may have pointed out that all criminal laws should have moral implications, so that the state can be seen as always appealing to values that are identifiable with the broadest of the mass population and gain the support of public opinion while raising the level of civilizing in support of the ruling class. The state's role is to gain organic continuity (SPN, 196). This represents achieving an equilibrium or a type of balance between the interests of the mass population that is identified as 'moral climate' or the general values of the beliefs of the majority of the mass population and the interests of the ruling class. This organic continuity, which must be maintained in order to maintain organized consent, cannot be seen as being dictated by unelected state officials such as the court. The gaining of this equilibrium or organic continuity is the role of government in general evident when interest of subgroups conflict with those of the ruling class. The discontent over the years of labour's interests in Canada is an example of this discontent or conflict and how the government had solved the issues through acts of legal coercion.

The historical significance of labour's struggles is evident in their attempt to gain acquisition of collective bargaining rights and a constitutionally recognized 'right to strike'. The struggles of the working class or labour has a long history in Canada. The ability for labour to organize and strike represents an attempt to balance the power relationship between labour and those that control the means of production. In 1956, a young Montreal lawyer, Pierre Elliot Trudeau provided a statement identifying the significance of a legally recognized right to strike on behalf of Canadian workers. According to Trudeau a strike or the threat of a strike:

> enables workers to negotiate with their employers on terms of approximate equality. It is wrong to think that unions are in themselves able to secure equality. If the right to strike is suppressed, or seriously limited, the trade union movement becomes nothing more than one institution among the many in the service of capitalism: a convenient organization for disciplining workers, occupying their leisure time, and ensuring their profitability for business-Pierre Elliot Trudeau (1956) (Panitch and Swartz, 25).

In another display of his acclaimed support for unions and their need for a legally recognized right to strike, in 1957 during a copper mine strike in Murdoch Ville, Trudeau during an interview with CBC identified the strength in numbers that unionized workers had as their own economic force (Trudeau, 1957). A labour strike symbolizes discontent with conditions of employment and the inability of these conditions to be reconciled with their employer. The ability to strike represents a balancing of power between labour and the

> the sheer scale flexibility, and durability, capital's material resources [that] continue to overwhelm those of labour, the organizational and ideological resources of labour remain scarcely measurable against the network of associations, organizations, advisory bodies, in-house publications, and mass media, which were owned by, or financially beholden to, capital and finally, capitals greater access to the state (Panitch and Swartz, 13).

The term capital as it is used by Panitch and Swartz is a common phrase making reference to the Gramscian description of the dominant social group. Labour's ability to paralyze their employer's business operations through a strike provides the worker with the means to balance the power relationship between the two interests. The conception of the utility in possessing a right to strike is bound with the idea with labour's ability to achieve fair collective bargaining.

In response, to the illegal striking of the late 1800's the government of Canada began to change its approach from initiating the police to disrupt strikes to a more formal legal coercive approach. Legislation was passed by both the provincial and Parliamentary governments to create laws that were designed to institutionalize unions in an attempt to control the labour movement through regulations. Early on the controlling aspect of this new legislation began to support the suppression of labour's ability to strike enhancing the naturalization process that Litowitz describes as labour became disillusioned over time as to the level support that they would be offered by choosing unionization over militancy. The government and union representative's creation of unionization as a legally recognized private institution began in the late 1800's. Prior to this unions were illegal and any attempt made by labour to disrupt the modes of economic production was met with force by the state. The first form of the government's attempts at legal coercion to suppress labour's ability to strike came in the form of the *Trade Unions Act* of 1872. Enacted by Parliament, it provided the first form of legal recognition of unions, preventing some of its members from going to jail in the event of a strike. It did not provide any form of positive rights for labour in the form of collective bargaining and governments still continued to employ the police to break up striking that was still considered illegal. A major shift towards labour rights seemed to have occurred on February 17, 1944 as the Dominion or federal government of Canada adopted War time labour relation legislation that continued until 1948. This legislation enacted by the liberal government under Prime Minister William Lyon Mackenzie King, legally recognized the right of workers to engage into collective bargaining agreements but what constituted a legal strike was still not addressed.

This seemed to be a new era of ideology and this legislation was soon adopted by all the provinces. According to John Godard in his paper *A Historical-Institutionalist Perspective,* this legislation was based on the Wagner model of the United States.

> Until the early twentieth century, freedom of contract was the dominant legal ideology in the US. It assumed that workers as individuals were on an equal footing with their employers and did not want collective representation, so it

> envisaged little or no legal basis for such
> representation or for other forms of
> voice at work. The Wagner Act was
> supposed to depart from that ideology
> by giving workers a right to self-
> organization, but from the very
> beginning the cards were stacked against
> that right (Godard 397).

The duty to bargain in good faith was a fundamental precept of the Wagner model. If the Canadian government is supposed to represent the interests of the Canadian people it must find a way to balance its support for both the country's economy and the interests of the labour force through support of collective bargaining rights. According to Giuseppe Vacca, "there is no hegemony without democracy" (Riley, 3). Thinking of how representative government is supposed to function, social change can be achieved through two mechanisms of the state: the courts and voting. Scholars who advocate this democratic interpretation of Gramsci's theory tend to present his *Prison Notebooks* as a sharp break with Lenin's ideas about the state and revolutionary strategy (Riley 2).

Gramsci describes the individual members of that state as the 'collective man' who are part of collective life to conceptualize the idea of how relationships between individuals and beliefs interact together within state. The 'collective man' (possibly Gramsci may have used wording in this way so that his notes were easily passed through the jail guards but this is unknown) or collective individual represents someone who consents to adhering to the imposed level of civilizing of the state. Together these individuals form collective life sharing this common belief. According to Gramsci, "the collective man presupposes cultural-social unity where different wills, and aims are together based on an equal and common conception of the world and this represents a collective attaining a single cultural climate" (SPN, 349). There exists some underlining foundation to the variety of belief systems within civil society that maintains a cultural climate. This for Gramsci refers to the level of civilizing and the abstract values or principles that underline the law where most of the mass population agrees on some essential values that support the level of civilizing. Then each collective individual experience a way of life in the state by modifying their behaviors according to the laws and support of the dominant ideology. This does not mean that there are not different sets of beliefs within the collective but that there their might be a multitude of different sets of beliefs but the behaviors of the collective conform and their beliefs are modified to support the level of civilizing of the state. Through the creation of laws, the mass population conforms their beliefs to resemble that there are certain behaviors that they should conform to in their daily lives to avoid breaking the law. This is formulated into some general understandings of how they conduct themselves in relation to others and this is what Gramsci describes as collective life. Some of those individuals who commit crimes are pressured to reintegrate themselves back into society or back into becoming a 'collective man'. So, those who do not follow the law represent those who choose not to conform to the level of civilizing by the state and do not represent actions that are part of the collective life or a collective man.

Achieving organic continuity represents the state's ability to use coercion to balance the interests of subgroups with the interests of the ruling class. "[The] collective man finds a means to integrates themselves into the collective life, thereby contributing to the collective life through the support of their own collaboration" (SPN, 242). This is done willingly by the individuals (SPN, 242). The majority of the mass population involves themselves in physically and mentally contributing to these economic forces, thereby involving themselves in furthering the interests of the ruling class. For example, the modes of productive forces require workers and these workers engage in labour that serves to support the modes of production. Labour also consents to follow the policies and laws that govern relationships between them and their employers. Labour by agreeing to unionization in the early 1900 in Canada, consents to follow the system of laws and regulations designed by the state in the course of how grievances are to be resolved, as well as consenting to follow contractual agreements that they are involved in with their employer that imposes various obligations.

Labour by unionizing consented to a part of the collective life and to the level or civilizing that unionization represented. Each individual member of unionized labour that was illegally involved in striking pre-unionization has now willingly integrated themselves into collective life by unionization in Canada. In this way the discontent or cultural climate of labour as a subgroup that initially acted against authority to achieve their goals was quelled legally through the institutionalization of labour. Gramsci discusses leadership as having to be able to recognize the cultural climate of the collective in arriving at organic continuity (SPN, 196). It is state's role to create social conformism which is useful to the ruling groups line of development and settle any conflicts preferably through legal means

(SPN, 195). The word legally is used by Gramsci to refer to the system of legal coercion. So, the institutionalization of labour stopped the progressions of collective striking. The threat was stopped before the cultural climate of the entire collective or collective life became affected through the acts of illegal striking of labour that could have changed the views of all members of collective life or every subgroup. Therefore, before labour became a real threat to authority, the government's solution to the problem was to unionize labour, providing them with concessions through legal means that allowed the state to integrate those collective labour forces who willingly defied authority by illegally striking into collective life consenting to the directives of leadership.

This new sense of order or civilizing gave both sides mechanisms to mediate instead of resorting to striking. The courts could then pressure unions, unionized labour and to the mass population to reinforce these newly established laws that were supposed to support the values by which labour was recognized. The educative pressure (Gramsci is not specific but it might be that he is referring to all forms of educative pressures within the superstructure) assists at incorporating the single individual into the collective (SPN, 242). Unionization was sold as a means to achieve the goals of labour dictating a new relationship between labour and their employers. The pressure that was applied through the courts is to support the legal principle that labour had to conform to the new regulations or laws that outlined this new relationship between labour and their employer. The underlining values that Labour though that the new regulations were to support is another issue because as time progressed the state reinterpreted and developed the laws which did not support these values. According to Gramsci "when a struggle can be resolved legally, it is certainly not dangerous; it becomes so when the legal equilibrium is recognized to be impossible" (SPN, 257). It is only when conflicts between subgroups within the state cannot be solved legally do they pose a threat to authority and therefore hegemony. The government does it utmost to resolve these conflicts through laws and the courts. Often the result of these outcomes is that the government provides some forms of concessions to these subgroups. These concessions often appear as if the subgroup has gained some ground with their demands while the state continues to find alternatives or works to incorporate these concessions into how they raise the level of civilizing in support of the interests of the ruling class over time. For example, some of these concessions while they remain active for a short period of time the government or through private institutions in civil society erode or replace them with alternatives that diminish the effects that these concessions have in how they may work against the interests of the ruling class. In other words, they only serve to quell the immediate potential threat to authority until enough time has passed and this potential threat to authority has greatly diminished; new forms of coercion can take their place to serve the interests of those that control the modes of productive forces.

While the new legislation recognizing collective bargaining seemed to be a step in the right direction for labour it only served to strengthen the governments control over labour as time went on. In 1946, Mr. Justice Rand was appointed official arbitrator in a civil dispute involving workers and the Ford Motor company in Windsor Ontario. Justice Rand handed down his decision that should have the effect of changing the landscape of labour rights. According Panitch and Swarts summarizing Justice Rand:

> [against] the consequence of that, as the history of the past century has demonstrated, the power of organized labour the necessary copartner of capital, must be able to redress the balance of what is called social justice; the just protection of all interests in an activity which the social order approves and discourages (Panitch and Swartz, 11).

Considered a land mark decision at the time by some, Justice Rand recognized the necessity of the workers to balance the playing field between themselves and their employers. The initial reaction of this ruling was" positive and with the implementation of the 1948 passing of the Industrial Relations and Disputes Investigations Act by the Federal government, accompanied by similar provincial legislation signified that legal protection of workers' freedom to organize and bargain" (Panitch and Swartz, 15). What was happening was that the governments were looking at different ways to control labour's ability to strike by pushing unions to adopt new labour contract agreements that would impede the future ability to strike.

The first attempt at thwarting advancements of the labour movement began shortly after the Rand decision. The Canadian courts began to take a more active position in the struggle of the workers through legislation and contractual agreements. The Rand ruling while it was a jump in the right direction for labour's rights, the government it seemed was hard at work for the other side. After, Rand [coercion] in capital-labour relations became less ad hoc and arbitrary: as the state's rationalization and institutionalization of workers' freedoms of association became more formal, so did coercion. What before had taken the appearance of the charge of the Mounties now increasingly took the form of the rule of law by which unions policed themselves in most instances. Where they did not the courts-with most Canadian judges all too rarely following Rand in his sagacity or sense of social justice- were often quick to act with injunctions and additional restrictions on picketing that reflected a judicial perpetuation, alongside the new legal framework, of tradition of ad hoc interventions to the benefit of capital Panitch and Swartz, 15).

Excluding Ontario, the other provinces chose not to follow the ruling of Rand, nor were they legally bound to follow the decision. What occurred more rapidly during this era, soon after the Rand decision, was the implementation of ambiguously worded labour agreements. Employers aimed to control labour through legal means. In many instances labour was forced into signing new forms of contract agreements designed by lawyers representing employers and governments to inhibit the workers ability to exercise their ability to legally strike. These forms of contract agreements became the new form of legal coercion protected and enforced by the state, in both the private and public employment sectors. The Rand decision did not force other provinces to fall in line and it would take a ruling on collective bargaining rights by the Supreme

Court of Canada to force other provinces and the federal governments into uniformity. Unions began entering into agreements with employers that all too often placed the union itself as the official police of their members; placing their leadership in jeopardy of criminal prosecution for non-compliance of provisions in labour contracts. Often unions were at odds with their members because of new contract agreements. These agreements were vague, and placed future collective bargaining attempts at risk.

As the legislation intensified its control over labour's ability to strike and to engage in fair arbitration, so did the penalties for transgressing the law that regulated labour. In the public sector, as soon as a dispute would arise, creating the potential of a general strike, it became common for "governments [to] introduce such legislation with greater dispatch and less parliamentary debate, including increasingly onerous penalties for defiance of the law" (Panitch and Swartz, 27). If a strike would ensue the governments implemented a new tactic in the 1950's called 'back to work legislation'. This legislation,

> characterized the government's policy towards labour marking a shift the generalized rule of law form of coercion where the legal framework establishes and constrains the rights and powers of all unions towards a selective state coercion where the state removes for a period, specific rights contained in labour legislation (Panitch and Swartz, 27).

This was designed by the government to "contain and suppress manifestations of class conflict as practiced within the institutionalized freedom of association. The rhetoric was that emergency powers of the government had to be invoked. (Panitch and Swartz, 28). Breaking down the amounts of back to work legislation since the 1950 to the early 1980's:

- 1950 -1965: back to work legislation: 6 instances both at federal and provincial level of back to work legislation
- 1950 first back to work legislation against "railway workers striking for a 40-hour week and pay increases prime minister St. Laurent said the welfare and security of the nation were imperiled (Panitch and Swartz, 27).
- Back to work legislation, there was fifty-one instances in the 15 years since 1965 half came in 1975 -1979.
- 1980-1984: Back to work legislation twenty-two legislative measures

(Panitch and Swartz, 27).

Governments were providing legal justification to have workers barred from striking. The arguments on both sides were equally compelling; on one hand, labour argued that they could not be forced to work under conditions of employment that were unfavorable and the government argued that it needed to function.

One interesting historical piece of early 'back to work' legislation placed the union leaders at risk of jail if they did not properly notify their own union members of the legal implications of an illegal strike or wild cat strike. A strike that is not legal in the sense that, the government has place restrictions on striking (or subsequent labour contracts have restricted striking) is called a wild cat strike. Different governments both provincial and Federal had placed specific clauses in their respective legislation holding the union heads accountable for these wild cat strikes if they were to occur. The purpose of this legislation or legal coercion was to place the policing of potential illegal actions of disgruntled unionized workers in the responsibility of the leaders of the union, making it a criminal act by omission. According to the legal definition of negligence the "doctrine of *negligence* rests on the duty of every person to exercise due care in his or her conduct towards others from which injury may result" (Blacks, 1032). *Culpable negligence* which is a type of negligence, is the failure to exercise that degree of care rendered appropriate by the circumstances, and which a man of ordinary prudence in the same situation and with equal experience would not have omitted" (Blacks, 1033). In 1978 J.C. Parrot a union leader, "was charged for remaining silent and not encouraging his members not to defy the back-to work legislation. He was charged for not publicly urging union members to obey the law" (Panitch and Swartz, 28). This is an example Litowitz description of rationalization; the rise of functionary intellectuals as union representatives who promote the system of governance of labour. His conviction for his omission was mitigated by the fact that he admitted to the fact that he remained silent and did not warn union member of the ramifications to their actions. The problem with enforcing such legislation is that even if Mr. Parrot had simply said that he was under the understanding that those individual workers were already made aware that they were not supposed to engage in a wild cat strike or if he provided a mere warning too them verbally or in written form, his actions may not have necessarily averted the potential for danger. Where is the public harm? Or can this be easily coerced into the common-sense argument that, in the public's interest to avoid the need for police involvement in 'braking up' a strike that might place those striking and the police in danger? Similar back to work legislation existed prior to Mr. Parrots conviction but went unnoticed or ignored by the government (Panitch and Swartz, 28).

The third form of major legislation directed at controlling labour's ability to strike by the Canadian government came in the form of wage control legislation that was in effect from 1975-1978. According to Mark Thompson in his paper, *Public Sector Industrial Relations in Canada: Does It Threaten or Sustain Democracy?* the general understanding of how public-sector workers would be regulated up until now was that

> a general model of labor relations legislation ... include workers' right to choose to join a union and engage in collective bargaining. Negotiations can encompass a wide variety of subjects (though more limited than private sector bargaining); unions in most bargaining units can strike, and employers can lockout workers. Collective agreements regulate the workplace in detail. Enforcement of these agreements is through private arbitration. A separate administrative agency (commonly called a "labor relations board") regulates the system (Thompson, 396).

The 1970's saw a large number of wild cat strikes as a result of the unions inability to address the issues of their members. The biggest strike in North American history happened in Quebec in 1972 when 300,000 employees walked off their jobs. With the high price of oil and dismal global economic outlook, Canada by 1974 had an unprecedented inflationary rate that the liberal government of Trudeau saw the situations as having the ability to destroy Canada's international economic position. Parliament was convinced that they had to do something but they had no clear plan on how to prevent the problem. In 1975, Parliament adopted the new Anti-Inflation Measures Act that, among other restraints they had implemented, had the effect of weakening unions. According to Panitch and Swartz

> the statutory incomes policy of the *Anti-Inflation Program* of 1975-78 suspended collective bargaining for all workers, initiated by the government and upheld by the courts on the basis of an elastic definition of economic emergency where the aspect of the policy entailed only wage controls (Panitch and Swartz, 28-29).

The liberal government of Trudeau was involved in the promotion of liberal reform at this time representing a stanch separation from the ideology of the liberal government of 1944 under the War time labour relations legislation. This is an example of an appeal to universalization of Litowitz, by Trudeaus government.

Gramsci describes how the state either creates new law or adapts existing law to apply to the needs of the ruling class. According to Gramsci "the goal of the state is to continuously adapt the "civilizing and the morality of the broadest popular masses to the necessities of the continuous development of the economic apparatus of production" (SPN, 242). This is the hegemonic function of political society. The way this is achieved seems to imply that Gramsci was referring to majoritarianism but it might also mean that the majority standard is where law makers derive their values. It is also where the state bases their oral defense upon the enactment and application of the level of civilizing that they intend to achieve. According to Gramsci,

> every state is ethical in as much as one
> of its most important functions is to
> raise the great mass of the population to
> a particular cultural and moral level, a
> level (or type) which corresponds to the
> needs of the productive forces for
> development, and hence to the interests
> of the ruling class (SPN, 258).

Gramsci uses the word as raising the level of civilizing because what the state is doing is building upon certain legally pre-established values that are the foundations upon what some existing laws have been based upon. These values can include an established conception of the law.

This era's political ideology, placed the economic problems of the country on the backs of labour. The choice that was confronting labour was that their actions had to support accepting the continued suspension of their collective bargain gains that they made over the years, and refrain from any form of striking in support of the dominant ideology. According to M. Mandel,

> [in] the context of three interconnected
> contemporaneous phenomenon: the
> expansion of suffrage, the deep
> involvement of the state in the economy,
> and the increasing tendency to
> malfunction of Western industrial
> economies. Legalized politics can be
> seen as a defense mechanism developed
> to preserve the status quo of social
> power from the threats posed by these
> phenomena (M. Mandel 82).

The entire struggle of labour's attempts for fair collective bargaining can be summarized as something that was dealt with legally. While labour's need was to obtain job security they always wanted to work and obtain a living. This enabled the coercive forces of the state to transform labour. This historically development is an example of how new laws may be initially accepted out of fear or self-interest but then later become the accepted norm of society. Labour began to adapt to unionization and regulations to seek relief from their grievances with their employers.

The government of Canada was not alone in the promotion of their liberal ideology. They were "aided, implicitly at least, by a bevy of industrial relations experts" (Panitch and Swartz, 31). Trudeau's 1975-78 Anti-Inflation program

> only involved effective wage restraint, adding that for economic (the openness of Canadian economy) and political (capitalist objections, the evils of bureaucracy) reasons, such programs can do no more than restrain incomes. [Trudeau did not] view wage increases as the sole cause of inflation. Nonetheless, he commended controls (if not the governments lack of candor) to labour, arguing that it was in labour's interest to acquiesce to such policies (Panitch and Swartz, 31).

This it reveals exactly one of the conceptions of the law that was used to maintain organizing consent: acquiescence, by making the dominant groups interests appear to be universal interests. The interest of the dominant social group was not liberal doctrine but through an appeal of liberal doctrine their interests were being promoted by government. Trudeau presented

Canadians with reasoning or conception under the implementation of the new legislation why such measures were important at the time were in the best interests of labour. In his appeal, Trudeau hoped to draw support for Parliamentary action. He utilized the laws outlining the limitations on labour, placing restrictions on the rights of labour. Trudeau aimed to invoke their common sense of labour that these measures would be in their best interests. In reality, the effect of this legislation could not affect the stop of inflation, nor did it prevent the recession that was felt in 1981-82. Yet the same rhetoric was used to implement coercive state intervention during the 1980's (Panitch and Swartz, 32). It was another attempt to utilize the law to place limits and controls through enforcement on the labour's ability to strike. By the 1980's the economic situation of Canada was worsened. By 1981 the inflations rate was at an all-time high at 11 percent, businesses were losing faith in the system and unemployment figures were on the rise.

Liberal ideology, from its early adoption in Canada continues to resonate today. According to W.A. Bogart in his book Courts and the Country, in Canada the dominant liberal ideology is a part of the judiciary (Bogart, 8). The "veneration of individualism, including protecting economic and property rights, has often dominated the judge's decisions" (Bogart, 8). This does not mean that the courts only employ one variance of liberal ideology but that they tend to employ reference to a certain set of liberal values in their decision making. With the advent of the ideology of liberalism, the judiciary expanded the common law to reflect liberal ideals" (Greene, 10). This is the conception of the law that was created in Canada. In *Ontario (Attorney General) v. Fraser* [2011] SCC 3, one of the main issues raised was regarding collective bargain rights of the Ontario farm workers and the *Agricultural Employees Protection Act, 2002* ("*AEPA*") which excluded farm labour's from the *Labour Relations Act* ("*LRA*") that promoted collective bargaining for labour. According to the Supreme Court of Canada in their reasoning in this case: "[the] Court is founded on precedents and their rulings must be consistent with the values of Canada" (*Ontario (Attorney General) v. Fraser* [2011] SCC 3). Some of these values represent liberal ideology but its anyone's guess what all of the values of Canada might be. The Court found that the AEPA did contravene section 2(d), a finding in favor of farming; the comment by Justice Abella whose husband was a stanch labour advocate at one time, that the Court is premised both on precedents and values of Canada shows that the ability of the Court to draw on abstract principles in all of its decisions. While the Court follows precedents, it does not have to follow precedents all of the time, which means that they can change their interpretation of the values of Canada and similarly, Charter values that are also representative of the values of Canada. The Supreme Court of Canada is not bound to follow their own decisions, as was clear in *Saskatchewan Federation of Labour v. Saskatchewan,* [2015] SCC 4. The law is not to viewed in a vacuum, it changes and develops as societal concerns change which is the reasoning why the Court has this ability to determine what these values are and how they are to be applied.

Chapter six:
Coercion and the *Charter*:

Gramsci makes direct reference to constitutional law in the prison notebooks, describing how certain entrenched values must remain abstract to aid in the state's ability to arrive at organic continuity. Gramsci defined the constitution as "the legal form of the state together with its institutions" (SPN, 212). What is codified in the constitution is the legal description of state relationships between the mass population and the institutions of government and the -relationships between inter-governmental institutions. Constitutions generally express's rights that are protected from government intervention. These are express guidelines that the government must follow, placing restraints on government action and defining the general structure of the government. In Canada, a constitutional monarchy, the constitution is not just one formal document and constitutional law can be drawn upon different legal documents such as the Charter and different decisions in common law. Gramsci describes a true constitutional governance neither rules or truly governs, it is the people that govern themselves (SPN, 253). A hegemonic government works to support the interests of the ruling class that dominates. Gramsci describes that a form of hegemonic government can only place abstract principles within its constitution for this reason (SPN, 253). It is only through an appeal to these abstract values that can be broadened to support the interests of the ruling class that enables the state to "balance the [two] interests in civil society" (SPN, 253). This form of appeal works to balance these two interests. It aids in the government's ability (and the state in general that comprises both the political and civil institutions who echo the same appeals) to be perceived as representing the people while it works to support the interests of the development of the economic productive forces. Gramsci was concerned with the ability of leadership to maintain the long-standing regime of the ruling class. According to Gramsci "subgroups whose interests vary and are not excusive" (SPN, 253). Constitutional values by remaining abstract allow for different interpretations and means of applications to different circumstances. The courts as can the legislatures justify raising the level of civilizing in support of the interests of the ruling class by interpreting abstract values rather than being held to the letter of the law. In civil systems the legislatures make this appeal solely. Gramsci did not seem to make reference to the ability of the courts to interpret the abstract values of law, only how the legislatures might appeal to these abstract values in incorporating the interests of the ruling class in the creation of new laws. In Canada, the reference process and the ambiguity in the wording of rights as they were drafted in the Charter aids in the coercion of the state to gain organic continuity.

Canadian constitutional law, involves prescribed rights and freedoms that are codified in the Charter, which every other law created by common law or enacted, must not infringe upon unless saved under section 1. Referring back to this quote by Gramsci, he notes that "it is not possible to create constitutional law of the traditional type on the basis of this reality, which is in continuous movement; it is only possible to create a system of principles asserting that the states goal is its own end, is own disappearance, in other words the re-absorption of political society into civil society" (SPN, 253). The reality that Gramsci is referring to is the idea that the government serves the interests of the ruling class. A codified constitution cannot hold directions on how every conflict in the state is to be resolved legally, nor can it solve the solutions to intrinsically political matters. While Gramsci identifies that there is no predetermined way to create laws he is also saying that there is no predetermined way of governing in how to achieve organic continuity. The state is continuously, adapting to a changing economic landscape and must adapt its laws to accommodate this transition, therefore in constant state of disequilibrium. Further, Gramsci is not advocating the democratic legitimacy of elected officials but is identifying, while political society tries to gain organic continuity that it must appear to be working on behalf of the interests of the mass population to gain their consent. The courts and the elected officials each represent the interests of the development of economic forces. Therefore, they must work together to advance the interests of the ruling class while at the same time serve to transform the mass population or the collective life to support this goal. These institutions of political society in part achieve this support by extending the existing rights to the development of economic productive forces. For example, in Canada corporations enjoy much of the same rights and protections from government intrusion as the individual person. This in turn provides more freedoms of the economic forces of production.

The Canadian governments involvement in the economy from the late 1900's to the new-found era of the Charter in the early 1980's was characteristic of leaderships support for the interests of the dominant social group. The Canadian economy has been supported through constant economic regulation by the government and historically with the depression of the 1930's. By the second world war the Canadian government aided the dominant social groups relentless exploitation of labour, that continued through the Charter era (M. Mandel, 82). By the time of the Charter according to M. Mandel,

> government spending in support of private enterprise and non-corporate welfare had approached fifty percent of the Gross National expenditure (GDE). State sector workers accounted for perhaps one-quarter of the labour force. This has been constant and increasing source of annoyance and concern to the most powerful, that is to say, the wealthiest, sectors in society, namely business, big and small, not only for the immediate interference with profit making it poses, but for long-term consequences of popular control of the economy (M. Mandel, 83).

Michael Mandel cites the lack of interest that big business has and continues to have for government involvement into the economy, unless it's advantageous of big business. The interest of the dominant social group is that the economy is a private affair not to be regulated by governments that can create potentially create obstacles to its goals.

Upon its patriation, the Charter has had a profound impact on the debate of labour rights in Canada. Unions, on behalf of labour, challenged the government's stance on back to work legislation claiming that they had a constitutionally protected right to strike under section 2(d) freedom of association. No member of the NDP at the time, the political party that claimed to represent labour's interests, believed that freedom of association under section 2(d) as expressed in the Charter represented a right to strike (M. Mandel 262). It was in plain sight, that a right to strike was not explicitly written in the form of a right within the Charter. According to Michael Mandel

> the unions put forwards court challenges that were wide ranging created by the opposition to back to work legislation and the 1982-83 restrictions on striking by various provincial and federal legislation such as the anti-inflation Act raged on over the years. The courts from all levels went back and forth on the issues, the courts were completely hostile "either "freedom of association did not include the right to strike (Public *Service Alliance of Canada*, 1984) or the restrictions on it we 'demonstrably justified' (Broadway Manor, Department Store Union, 1985) (M. Mandel, 263).

The advent of the Charter brought about a more litigious landscape in Canada. Section 2(d) stated that there was a freedom of association and it was up to the courts to decide if this referred to a right to strike. The ambiguity under section 2(d) and the issue of a right to strike would seemingly only be settled by the Supreme Court of Canada because the lower superior courts of the provinces were all mixed on the issues.

Purposively, some rights and freedoms were drafted under the Charter with ambiguous language that begs interpretation from the courts. According to the chief Justice of Canada Beverly McLachlin the role of the Courts

> at its most basic, it is to decide legal disputes that citizens and the government ask them to decide. In deciding these disputes, the Courts discharge a number of functions essential to democratic governance. First, they define the precise contours of the division of legislative powers between the federal and provincial governments. Second, they rule on legislation alleged to be unconstitutional for violation of the *Charter*, and in doing so define the scope of constitutional rights and freedoms. Third, the courts exercise *de facto* supervision over the hosts of administrative tribunals created by Parliament and the Legislatures (Government Canada, 2017).

The ambiguity in the language of the Charter begs the court's interpretation giving rise to the Court ability to define constitutional law often broadening or narrowing certain interpretations of rights and freedoms. This has a direct effect of the level of desired civilizing by the state. Owen Fiss in his paper *Equal Protection Clause*, suggested that by placing specific rather than ambiguous wording in the constitution can often better serve to protect individuals or group interests [16]. Centered around issues in America concerning discrimination, the intension of Fiss was to remove the ability of state Superior Courts from moving away from federally enacted laws that prohibited discrimination. He suggested placing specific wording within the American constitution through amendment to protect African Americans, to ensure their protection from ambiguous interpretations and appeals to other substantiated constitutional values that would work to invalidate the federal laws designed to prohibit discrimination. His argument was that a group-disadvantaging principal was a" better claim to represent the ideal of equality" (Fiss, p-85). It would be better, according to Fiss if the state wanted constitutional protection of a right or a freedom to have it specifically worded into the constitution. Fiss identifies in his paper, the problems that arise and are associated with leaving constitutional wording too abstract. There are inherent advantages and disadvantages to leaving some rights to the courts to either narrow or broaden, but the general idea of how this relates to Gramsci's conception is how it enables the state to manipulate wording to raise the level of civilizing in favor of the interests of the ruling class.

The debate of whether labour had a constitutionally protected right to strike under the Charter reached the Supreme Court in 1987. At issue was the constitutional status of collective bargaining and the right to strike. There were three-separate appeals made:

> (1) Government of Saskatchewan v. Retail. Wholesale and Department Store

---

[16] I have an email from Owen Fiss that confirms this assertion.

Union (Retail, Wholesale and department Store Union, 1987), the Saskatchewan dairy workers case; (2) Public service Alliance of Canada v. queen (Public Service Alliance of Canada, 1987, the Challenge to federal public-sector wage control legislation and (3) Re Public Service Employee relations Act (Alberta) (1987), a reference by the Alberta government on various restrictions on collective bargaining in the Alberta public services, substituting limited compulsory arbitration for the right to strike in the case of public service employees , fire fighters, hospital employees, and police officers (M. Mandel, 264).

The ruling of the Court was that under freedom of association there existed no express right to strike. The Court had three positions and four opinions, with four to two against the right to strike (M. Mandel, 264). By not providing a constitutionally recognized right to strike the Court was maintaining the status quo. It seemed that labour in losing this fight served the interests of those that controlled the modes of production.

This seemed to change when the Court reversed their decision in 2015. Constitutional text can be changed by the Court without changing its written content. According to Richard Albert in his paper, *How Unwritten Constitutional Norms Change Written Constitutions,* the

> [written] constitutions may also change

> informally. An informal change occurs where the enforceable meaning of the constitution changes without altering the constitutional text. For instance, where courts possess the power of judicial review, and where that power is effective, the functionally binding quality of a national court of last resort interpreting the constitutional text approximates the formally binding quality of a written constitutional amendment. The form of entrenchment may differ but their effects are largely indistinguishable. This is the sense in which a written constitution may be altered informally. Judicial interpretation is only one such method. There are others, including legislative enactment and executive action. (Albert, 3)

The Supreme Court of Canada because there is not expressed written right to strike under Sec 2(d) of the Charter, they can alter the interpretation of a freedom of expression when ever they see fit. The Court applied a new value in 2015, a value that had been echoed by labour since the late 1800's. The Court was able to redefine the parameters of freedom of association by appealing to a new system of values and not by changing the words in the Charter. This leads to wonder if the Court will change their minds in the future. According to Justices McLachlin C.J. and LeBel, Abella, Cromwell and Karakatsanis J.J:

> [the] right to strike is an essential part of a meaningful collective bargaining process in our system of labour

relations. The right to strike is not merely derivative of collective bargaining, it is an indispensable component of that right. Where good faith negotiations break down, the ability to engage in the collective withdrawal of services is a necessary component of the process through which workers can continue to participate meaningfully in the pursuit of their collective workplace goals. This crucial role in collective bargaining is why the right to strike is constitutionally protected by s. 2(*d*) (*Saskatchewan Federation of Labour v. Saskatchewan*, [2015] SCC 4).

The flip flop of the Court on the issue of a right to strike affirms the abstractness of certain principles of justice that allow the Court to pick and choose what principle may apply or when they may apply it and how they may apply it.

Twice labour had appealed to the Charter to secure their self-proclaimed right to strike. What had changed was that the Court decided to appeal to a new set of principles in their interpretation of section 2(d), the same set of principles that labour valued. Subgroups have often sought redress through litigation as a means of societal change.

> The liberal 'myth of rights' is the view that those suffering disadvantage should seek redress by striving to have their

> grievances protected by securing legal recognition of their claim as a right. Once a right is recognized, whether by constitutions, legislations, or judicial decision, all those whose rights are threatened or denied may approach the relevant court and have their rights enforced, attaching litigation, rights and remedies with social change" (Hunt, 309)

According to Hunt "faith in the instrumental value and utility of rights forms the political common sense of the age" (Hunt, 309). This is how the Charter was sold to the Canadian public: that constitutionally protected rights would be created to prevent government intrusion and the courts would ensure that these rights were protected. Moreover, constitutional norms were intended as a direct legal basis of individual rights and obligations. (Bashiera, 291). This form of redress through Charter challenges is not something that is available to everyone. The high costs that are associated in making constitutional challenges make it out of reach for the majority of the population.

With means to afford the constitutional challenge, unions made a successful advancement of labour rights in 2015. The liberal landscape appeared to change with the recognition of a constitutionally protected right to strike under freedom of association. Overturning their previous decision on the right to strike the Supreme Court of Canada in 2015 recognized that a right to strike was constitutionally recognized under freedom of association section 2(d). Two sets of legislation were at issue for the Court, *The Public Service Essential Services Act*, S.S. 2008, c. P-42.2 (PSESA), and *The Trade Union Amendment Act*, 2008 S.S. 26, which became law in May, 2008. In *Saskatchewan Federation of Labour v. Saskatchewan,* [2015] SCC 4, the Supreme Court found that:

> [in] July 2008, the Saskatchewan Federation of Labour and other unions challenged the constitutionality of both the PSESA and The Trade Union Amendment Act, 2008. The trial judge concluded that the right to strike was a fundamental freedom protected by s. 2(d) of the Canadian Charter of Rights and Freedoms and that the prohibition on the right to strike in the PSESA substantially interfered with the s. 2(d) rights of the affected public-sector employees. He also found that the absolute ban on the right to strike in the PSESA was neither minimally impairing nor proportionate and therefore was not saved by s. 1 of the Charter. The declaration of invalidity was suspended for one year. On the other hand, the trial judge concluded that the changes to the certification process and permissible employer communications set out in The Trade Union Amendment
>
> Act, 2008 did not breach s. 2(d). (*Saskatchewan Federation of Labour v. Saskatchewan* [2015] SCC 4)

The identification that freedom of association does

constitutionally protect a right to strike confers a negative right guaranteeing the governments non-interference. With the Courts flip flop that identifies the ambiguity present in the Charter that can lead to changes in the level of civilizing. The Court has now confirmed that there exists as a remedy to vindicate this right in the face of any infringement by government. The Court found that the provincial government of Saskatchewan failed on two thresholds if their legislation was to survive under section 1 of the Charter. The first was that they had to prove that the government service that was interrupted by a strike had to have been shown to be critical for the assurance of public safety. The second was that as soon as the government imposed the back to work legislation there had to have been enough time to formulate an agreement between management and labour. With this new recognition of a right to strike, labour has seemed to have won a victory that was claimed for over 60 years. This represents the Courts ability to bring constitutional text in line with social attitudes.

The implications of the Supreme Court of Canada's ruling, recognizing a right to strike, are still developing today. As Gramsci describes how necessities are turned into freedom; labour with the most recent Court ruling has had its necessity or what is felt it needed turned into a freedom by the Supreme Court. One implication is that the dominant social group has had 60 years to transform labour. It has seemingly removed the radical nature completely out of their movement. According to Michael Mandel, the ability of labour to strike showed,

> that workers have more power in association than they do individually.

> The only difference between individual
> and collective action is the relative
> effectiveness of the latter. The union
> movement caused a historic shift in the
> balance of power between labour and
> capital by the sheer act of combination.
> This called forth first the wrath of
> common law and then the compromise
> of collective bargaining legislation.
> Individual action has always been easily
> handled by the "silent compulsion of
> economic relations'. If there is any 'lack
> of analogy' involved here it is only the
> effectiveness of solidarity. But this
> according to liberal theory, is what
> "freedom of association" is supposed to
> protect (M. Mandel, 266).

Through regulation and contract agreements the ability to strike continues to be controlled legally. While there have been advancements in the form of concessions for labour there is no constitutional right to collective bargain (but then again how could there be, maybe the Court in the future will change this).

The Supreme Court of Canada recognizes that collective bargaining, as a process, ultimately rests in labour's ability to mediate with their employer. The Court decided that they will recognize the rights of labour in such a way as to ensure that government legislation does not impede with labour's ability to collectively bargain which takes its form in private mediation. What the Court did not say was that they would ensure that collective bargaining would occur. In Ontario (Attorney

General) v. Fraser, [2011] 2 S.C.R. 3, the Supreme Court found that:

> Section 2(d) of the Charter protects the right to associate to achieve collective goals. Laws or state actions that substantially interfere with the ability to achieve workplace goals through collective actions have the effect of negating the right of free association and therefore constitute a limit on the s. 2(d) right of free association, which renders the law or action unconstitutional unless it is justified under s. 1 of the Charter. This requires a process of engagement that permits employee associations to make representations to employers, which employers must consider and discuss in good faith (Ontario (Attorney General) v. Fraser, [2011] 2 S.C.R. 3).

There is no right to collective bargain that imposed upon another parties namely the employer to engage in collective bargaining. According to the Supreme Court of Canada in *Frasier* SCC [2011]:

> the reasons advanced in *Health Services* for extending protection to collective bargaining under s. 2(*d*) — Canadian labour history, Canada's international obligations, and *Charter* values — do not support conferring a constitutional right to collective bargaining and imposing a duty on employers to engage in collective bargaining.

The mistake that the Court of appeal made was that it interpreted section 2(d) of the Charter as imposing the right to collective bargaining upon the employer that the Supreme Court corrected. According to the Court

Second, s. 2(*d*) protects freedoms not rights. According to *Health Services*, if s. 2(*d*) protected only the ability of workers to make collective representations and did not impose a duty on the employer to bargain in good faith, it would fail to protect the right to collective bargaining. This proposition transformed s. 2(*d*) from a freedom into a positive right by imposing an obligation to act on third parties (i.e. the employer). A right to collective bargaining is also not derivative of a freedom — it is a standalone right created by the Court, not by the Charter . A derivative right is one that is necessary to allow individuals to exercise a fundamental freedom. No individual employee has a right to require an employer to meet and make a reasonable effort to arrive at an acceptable employment contract. To grant a right to collective bargaining under s. 2 (*d*) purportedly as derivative of the freedom of association is not consistent with the approach taken by this Court in its derivative rights jurisprudence in relation to the Charter (Ontario (Attorney General) v. Fraser, [2011] 2 S.C.R. 3.)

So, the right to collective bargaining as a standalone right does not impose a right or obligation to collective bargain upon the employer. What the Supreme Court has done, is recognize the right to collective bargain, as it has substantiated in *Frasier* SCC [2011], recognized that the right to strike as a balancing effect which recognizes the power that those who own the means of production have over labour. By securing the existence of a right to strike under the Charter, the Court recognized that the ultimate task of controlling labour is placed in the hands of the mediation process outside of the traditional court setting. This understanding of the importance of the mediation process and its effects was first introduced in this thesis paper by identifying the Rand decision; a decision rendered as a form of alternative dispute resolution or ADR.

The Supreme Court of Canada has recognized the advantages of successful mediation. *Health Services and Support – Facilities Subsector Bargaining Association v. British Columbia*, 2007 SCC 27 at paragraph 60:

> On the one hand, it [the *Wagner Act* model] granted major protections to workers to organize without fear of unfair interference from the employers and guaranteed workers the right to bargain collectively in good faith with their employers without having to rely on strikes and other economic weapons. On the other hand, it provided employers with a measure of stability in their relations with their organized workers, without the specter of intensive

state intervention in the economy ...
These elements ... continue to guide our
system of labour relations to this day.

And in *Dayco (Canada) Limited v. National Automobile, Aerospace and Agricultural Implement Workers Union of Canada (CAW-Canada)*, [1993] 2 S.C.R. 230, Justice Cory stated, at paragraph 93:

> Unresolved disputes fester and spread the infection of discontent. They cry out for resolution. Disputes in the field of labour relations are particularly sensitive. Work is an essential ingredient in the lives of most Canadians. Labour disputes deal with a wide variety of work related problems. They pertain to wages and benefits, to working conditions, hours of work, overtime, job classification and seniority. Many of these issues are emotional and volatile. If these disputes are not resolved quickly and finally they can lead to frustration, hostility and violence. Both the members of the workforce and management have every right to expect that their differences will be, as they should, settled expeditiously. Further, the provision of goods and services in our complex society can be seriously disrupted by long running labour disputes and strikes. Thus, society as a whole, as well as the parties, has an interest in their prompt resolution. (*Dayco (Canada) Limited v. National Automobile, Aerospace and Agricultural Implement Workers Union*

of Canada (CAW-Canada), [1993] 2 SCC 230).

The implications of the wording by Justice Cory implies a distinction between a cause for labour's action while noting a societal concern for the disruption of the modes of productive forces. This ignores the fact that there are significant societal concerns in relation to the needs of labour. In this case the Justice Cory only recognizes the concern that frustration can create to labour when the conflict that they may be involved in is not resolved quickly. The Court recognizes a need to resolve conflict effectively and refuse to enforce collective bargain on a third party's. The signal being sent by Justice Cory is that there is more of a concern for the disruptive force of a strike, over their concerns for a way of life that economic means can provide.

Prior to the mid 1900's the state recognized that labour's ability to organize and strike posed a threat to its authority. Gone unchecked, or if the state did not resolve the issue legally and arrive at organic continuity then the more power in numbers and thus organized that labour grew, as a force, it might have become it potentially could pose a threat to hegemony. According to Gramsci, "a crisis of authority is precisely the crisis of hegemony, or a general crisis of the State" (SPN, 210). Today with various legal coercive instruments in place the future of labour's ability to strike will most likely be dictated within the hands of the outcomes of ADR. Labour is coerced into contractual agreements with the threat of losing their jobs if they fail to agree to concessions. These contracts include mandatory arbitration prior to any strike can be initiated, estoppel clauses that limit their rights etc. These contractual clauses involving mandatory arbitration within the public sector have now become the norm; a practice adopted by every province in Canada as a part of their hiring procedure. This widespread use is not unique among the public sector but the private sector has adopted similar policies within their everyday business. For example, most cell phone agreements in Canada contain mandatory arbitration clauses and if there is any grievance with the wireless provider the is a clause in the contractual agreement that states prior to any civil action taken in traditional court there must be mandatory arbitration.

Chapter seven:
ADR and the pressures within the superstructure

Alternative dispute resolution mechanisms or ADR were initially embraced as a more cost effective and a more efficient process over the traditional court proceedings. This concept in law and policy underlines how ADR was promoted to the Canadian public. Trevor C. Farrow offers a glimpse into the world of ADR in his book entitled *Civil Justice, Privatization, and Democracy*. According to Farrow, ADR "may not be all that it is cracked up to be" (Farrow, 219). Different forms of ADR mediation include various mandatory court-based mediation rules, judicial dispute resolution initiatives, case management regimes, pre-trial conferences, cost-based settlement initiatives, etc., (Farrow, 5). Forms of ADR have also been adopted in the administrative system of traditional court including various tribunals such as landlord tenant, labour, in the criminal justice system and initiatives in the private sector such as negotiations, community-based dispute resolutions, etc., (Farrow, 5). These various forms of resolving conflict within the state involve less governmental restrains. This characteristic of ADR was implemented to promote a more efficient means by which parties could be encouraged to resolve their conflicts in a more open forum.

The Supreme Court of Canada has provided its support for ADR through different decisions that were intended to promote a less rigid form of conflict resolution. In one manner the Court has promoted that parties involved in ADR are not required by law to disclose details of an agreement reached by parties as a result of ADR mediation. In *Union Carbide Canada Inc. v. Bombardier Inc*, [2014] 1 SCC 800, the Court found that the use of confidentiality agreements was in keeping with the values of common law. Confidentiality, is a big part of ADR and at the risk of losing a party's monetary (or otherwise) settlement is a huge incentive for parties to remain quiet. By removing the government power of oversight, the law will not develop or be raised to support the interests of the mass population. Farrow argues, that ADR is having an eroding effect in terms of courts ability to make common law, arguing that the mass population is far better off when decisions are brought to light, helping the adjudication of future cases and development of common law (Farrow, 224). The traditional values of democracy as prescribed and interpreted under the Charter are jeopardized according to Farrow. Traditionally, developments made in legal decisions help to assist in bettering the role and ability of elected officials to create policy; to meet the needs of a changing society and the immediate interests of subgroups within the state. From another view point the rule of stare decisis or binding precedents by its rigidity, which binds inferior courts, may restrict judges from developing laws as well. But what Farrow is directing his argument towards is the fact that traditional courts are themselves a necessary feature of democracy in Canada, for their ability to create and develop laws that is not inherent in the process of ADR. Common law is also essential to the interests of subgroups who require government intervention to protect their interests. By reaffirming existing laws or new creating new *obiter dicta,* the courts aid in the policy making of elected officials is essential to what has become a fixture in understanding how democracy functions in Canada. So, it is important to note that the role of government in maintaining organized consent has promised certain protections to the mass population but as time wears on it seems as if in the interests of the ruling class governments allow for these protections to be circumvented.

Unlike traditional courts, mediators involved in the ADR process are allowed to rule in favor of one side's action without giving reasons for their position. This creates a lack of reference that would in traditional court potentially lead to questions of errors that may have occurred in law. If such an error had occurred in traditional court proceeding normally this would be sufficient grounds to have a matter, by motion, moved to appeal to question the outcome; almost automatically. This process of obtaining a successful appeal to traditional court from a decision that is rendered in ADR is very difficult to achieve. The Court has opted to place more importance on allowing decisions of mediators in ADR more control over the process than placing checks and balances over the process through government intervention. This lack of traditional government oversight, inherent in the ADR process, directly effects the fairness of the ADR process itself, which is something that traditional courts have long established within their process as imperative. How can litigants have assurances of a fair and proper decision being rendered if there is no oversight and enforcement of simple rules that are designed to provide assurances in the fairness of how these decisions are reached? Farrow suggests to counter this problem some form of co-operation or amalgamation of the public and private sector that will regulate the ADR process might solve this dilemma. In *Norman regional Health Authority vs. Manitoba Association of Health Care Professionals* [2011] 3 SCR 616, the court has ruled for limited court involvement in the ADR process. According Honorable Justice Fish J,

> to the broad mandate of arbitrators flows from the broad grant of authority vested in arbitrators by collective agreements, statutes such as *The Labour Relations Act* ("*LRA*"), and from their distinctive role in fostering peace in industrial relations. They are well equipped by their expertise to adapt the legal and equitable doctrines they find relevant within the sphere of arbitral creativity (*Norman regional Health Authority vs. Manitoba Association of Health Care Professionals*, [2011] 3 SCR 616).

Recognizing that the power of the mediator or arbitrator flowed mainly from contract, the Court's ruling in essence made it harder for any appeal to succeed from these private dispute mechanisms of ADR into traditional courts for review. By design ADR was promoted as a process that allowed a more open dialogue between parties, but this only served to remove required government oversights. Parties can mediate freely in ADR 'without prejudice' of having comments made in mediation that might have otherwise been used against them in possible future litigation in traditional court. But this created a problem of abuses in the process itself and questions now arise of fairness in the ability of parties to arrive at a fair resolution between both parties where fairness does not simply equate to a settlement reached.

Farrow raises the concern of the effect that the ADR process is having on democracy in Canada. The creation of laws and the ability of the courts to create common law that adapts to a changing society is a necessary feature of the Canadian role of governance. The function of traditional courts is to,
> resolve individual disputes, keep legislation in check through hearings, trials and judicial review, create a body of law that directly governs and indirectly guides-through the full light and shadow of common law, much of what we do in our daily lives, individual and corporate actors included. (Farrow, 252).

The ruling class is interested in control and constantly seeks new avenues to capitalize on this interest. The adjudicative system is "far from a simple mechanical dispute ending procedure playing a central role in the regulatory process of western democracy" (Farrow, 252). The Canadian system of democratic governance, according to Farrow, relies heavily on the adjudicative process for its authority and policy making function. According to Robinson,
> dominant social groups aim is intensive enlargement that involves the privatization of government businesses such as health care and the second extensive enlargement where capitalism is growing into places normally considered outside the normal area of capitalist production (Robinson, 8).

The expansion of capitalism happens through the commodification of social relation that include the means of capitalist production or commodity production. If social regulation becomes more privatized, society loses a part of public regulation. Farrow finds that ADR is having an eroding affect on Canadian democracy. Much of the effects of ADR go unseen because of the secrecy and lack of transparency that surrounds ADR. The future ramifications of less disputes being placed in the traditional courts to review remains to be seen in the short-term outcome. How democracy in Canada will adjust, if no implementations are introduced to curve or all together stop this lack of development of the law remains to be seen.

Public policy is potentially being taken away from government on a large scale by the expansion of ADR, placing it into the private sector. Public policy is often made through civil litigation in traditional court settings between different private disputes. The court exercises their powers of interpretation, often implementing forward thinking as to the implications of their rulings that they may have in a broader context. For example,

> if the conduct by the directors of a corporation is seen to oppress minority shareholders then theses same shareholders have recourse through the courts. The court will resolve the dispute, set ground rules through precedent setting for future expectations of actions by other directors in general (Farrow, 255).

Farrow cites the environmental damaged caused by the Enron oil spill in march 1989, and the *BCE Inc. v. 1976 Debenture holders* 2008 a Supreme Court of Canada decision that was about a leveraged buy-out deals where each case had additional concerns about how corporate law affects public interest. These concerns are often set in the wake of leading issues made by lawyers in live issues before the court. Successful class action suits "ensure that actual and potential wrongdoers modify their behaviors to take full account of the harm they are causing or might cause to the public" (Farrow, 257). For this reason it seems that the ruling class feels that its interests would be better served through the process of ADR where they can affect more control over the outcome (something that labour has echoed as the imbalance of power that the ruling class has over all other subgroups). In contrast a traditional court is instrumental in the application and creation of new laws that will determine and outline accepted actions in the state.

The final concern that Farrow's raises involves ADR and its relation to an understanding of globalization today. The Supreme Court of Canada has acknowledged that the "business of litigation, like commerce itself has become increasingly international" (Farrow, 263). Farrow's claim is that "international commercial actors pursue ADR to actively sidestep domestic process and often domestic [the state] substantive legal rights and obligations" (Farrow, 264). Those that control the means of productive forces in this sense would arguably rather less government regulation in the economy, as reflecting current liberal ideology. With more government oversight comes the potential of hindering their profit-making ability and with less government involvement in matters of litigation that would have the opposite effect. According to Gramsci,

> one can see how, when the impetus of
> progresses not tightly linked to a vast
> local economic development which is

> artificially limited and repressed, but is
> instead the reflection of international
> development which transmits their
> ideological currents to the periphery-
> currents born on the basis of the
> productive development of more
> advanced countries-then the group
> which is the bearer of new ideas is not
> the economic group but the intellectual
> stratum, and the conception of the State
> advocated by them changes aspect; it is
> conceived of as something in itself, as a
> rational absolute (SPN, 116-117).

Here Gramsci notes the importance of not confusing the dealings of intellectuals in the global economy with specific actions of a global dominant social group or global ruling class. Gramsci refers to how it may only seems as if there is one global order or how more developed countries have control over more underdeveloped countries but it is necessary to determine hegemony verses simple workings of intellectuals on an international scale who serve the interests of the ruling class of a particular nation-state. Many different scholars such as Robinson and possibly Farrow that have tried to identify global actors as a global ruling class. This attempt implies that Gramsci's theory of hegemony can be expanded in the international context, but without making the proper distinction between indirect actions of intellectuals and direct actions of a designated global ruling class, Gramsci's theory cannot be successfully applied. Before the theory of hegemony, as described by Gramsci, can be properly placed in a global context, first this distinction must be made.

ADR promotes the interests of the both the ruling class and the governments interests in obtaining organic continuity. By insulating themselves from government oversight, those that control the modes of economic production prefer utilizing ADR as it lessens the risk of potential harmful civil litigation. The government of Canada prefers that parties involved in disputes utilize the ADR process because it avoids issues that may be brought to light of public opinion that may cause problems in arriving at 'organic continuity'. Gramsci describes that every state "[tends] to create and maintain a certain type of civilization and of citizen (hence the collective life of individual relations), and eliminate certain customs and attitudes and to dismantle others, then the law will be its instrument for this purpose" (SPN, 246). Traditionally, legislatures and courts through common law have created relationships through the creation of laws historically to provide certain protections and benefits to mass population in Canada in raising the level of civility. ADR as an alternative institution of conflict resolution, circumvents the ability of some of these laws being applied. ADR allows for parties to be more secretive of their actions. This lack of transparency in ADR serves to shield those that control the modes of production, who prefer to use this form of conflict resolution, from litigation in traditional court. Political society can continue to raise the level of civilizing in support of the interests of the ruling class from the current level of civilizing without immediately worrying about the change in cultural climate that might arise out of litigation between conflicts of subgroups and those that control the modes of production when these conflicts are dealt with through the ADR process. According to Gramsci, these superstructure factors: structures of the state that support the existing economic forces, and for the state to create new structures that support the development of economic forces, "should not be left to themselves to develop spontaneously, to a haphazard and sporadic germination" (SPN, 247). The state will continuously support the interests of the development of economic forces through the law but the law should also continue to represent the interests of the mass population through their understanding of the underlining values of existing laws according to the level of civilizing that has currently been achieved by the state. By placing more conflict resolution in the hands of the private sphere without governmental monitoring it makes it more difficult on members of the mass population to have their rights protected from potential abuses that may occur from a result of the ADR process and the influence in the process from parties that own the modes of productive forces. By the utilization of ADR, the government of Canada is no longer portrayed as being limited by judicial constrains in how they civilize and create organic continuity. As Farrow points out, democratic values represent certain rights that protect individual liberty and the courts in Canada have a central role in protecting these rights.

Conflict resolution in Canada represents how both Kennedy and Litowitz describe Gramsci's theory of dominant order as being apparent at multiple levels. Some laws are designed to place checks and balances upon the conduct of the relationships in civil society. Parties that have more influence through monetary ability which are involved in the ADR process have more power to promote their own interests over others with this lack of government oversight. According to Gramsci the law,
> will have to be extended to include those
> activities which are presently classified

> as legal neutral, and which belong to the
> domain of civil society; the latter
> operates without sanctions or
> compulsory obligations, but never the
> less exerts a collective pressure and
> obtains objective results in the form of
> an evolution of customs, ways of
> thinking and acting morally (SPN, 242).

Different pressures emanate from civil society that influence individual behaviors. ADR is part of the pressure that emanates from civil society that are placed upon the individual or 'collective man' to conform to a certain way of thinking and acting. Farrow is unsure how societal norms may be affected in the future but it's possible that certain values that are currently held will be alter the development of Canadian society. According to Gramsci referring to the bourgeoisie class "it poses itself as an organism, capable of absorbing the entire society, assimilating it to its own cultural and economic level" (SPN, 260). Gramsci states that the "entire function of the state has been transformed then the state has become an educator" (SPN, 260). Therefore, that the intent of the ruling class may not be to secure the control of the mass population as Litowitz describes but it may be more accurate to say that Gramsci is describing it as a need to completely transform the mass population in order to control it. This description captures the idea of consent and removes the idea that control as a force could attain this transformation alone. Gramsci is identifying that the function of the state based upon the promotion of the interests of the ruling class and the willingness of the mass population to adopt the ideology that the ruling class promotes in order for them to obtain their goals. The law is a coercive instrument in attaining this goal. Continuously, by raising the level of civilizing the government works to transform the mass population towards supporting the interests of the modes of productive forces and therefore the ruling class. The Supreme Court of Canada because it supports organic continuity supports organized consent however the directives of the legislative government in support of the ruling class.

Chapter eight
The Nation State

There is currently extensive scholarly works devoted to applying Gramsci's theory of hegemony in the international context. Their efforts are focused on identifying either one or more dominant social groups in control of the global economic system of capitalism. One of the leading theories is that the expansion of capitalism globally has led to the transformation of nation-states into borderless countries where capital can flow freely throughout the globe and where the superstructure of both political and civil have been transformed under one collective dominant ideology of a dominant social group. Arguments ensue as to whether there are conglomerates of dominant social groups that have come together under one collective hegemony or there are competing dominant hegemonies fighting for control over the base structure. Antonio Gramsci's primary concern with respect to the powers within the state are tied to his theory of hegemony. William Robinson, describes the general understanding of a theory of hegemony as,

> "a concept developed by Gramsci that refers to the attainment by ruling groups of stable forms of rule based on consensual domination of subordinate groups. Gramsci's notion of hegemony posits distinct forms, or relations of domination: coercive domination and consensual domination. Hegemony may be seen as a relationship between classes or groups by gaining active consent. Hegemony is thus rule by consent, or the cultural and intellectual leadership achieved by a particular class, class fraction, stratum, or social group as part of a larger project of class rule or domination. It involves the

> internalization on the part of the
> subordinate classes of the moral and
> cultural values, the code of practical
> conduct, and the world-view of the
> dominant classes or groups, in sum the
> internalization of the social logic of the
> system of domination itself" (Robinson,
> 161).

The theory of hegemony presupposes a division of social groups where one dominant social group lead's over all other social groups. Leadership is secured through two means: the coercive apparatus of the state and by organized consent of subgroups. Robinson assembles Gramsci's theory of hegemony in one short paragraph capturing the essentials of how Gramsci viewed the nation state.

According to Gramsci, "the apparatus of the state's coercive power legally enforces discipline on those groups who do not consent either actively or passively" SPN, 12). Gramsci's 10-year incarceration, is an example of the Italian states legally enforcing such discipline. The trial of Gramsci was prompted by the Fascist government headed by Mussolini, initiated as a result of Gramsci simply speaking his mind. According to the popular consensus "Gramsci's trial, which began on 28 May 1928, was planned as a political showpiece. A special tribunal was convened to judge Gramsci and twenty-two other defendants for organizing an armed insurrection. Legal arguments and evidence were largely irrelevant-the regime had decided that a conviction was necessary, to be followed by exemplary punishment" (SPN, lxxxix). Politically motivated, Gramsci was on display as a revolutionary during the trial. He was labeled by the Italian prosecutor as someone who sought to destabilize the structure of the Italian state. Gramsci, a Marxist, was opposed to the ideals of Fascism describing it as a variant of capitalisms. "Nineteenth century historiography placed emphasis on the peculiarities which characterized different national legal experiences, thus closely adhering to the political purpose of strengthening national identities" (Baschiera, 284). The state placed ideological emphasis on the law to promote an importance on the value of national unity. One way for Mussolini to solidify his power was to simply remove opposition. In this case the court acted as the conduit for the promotion of Mussolini's own ideology, by forcing Gramsci out of politics as someone accused as a direct threat to the state authority. It is not difficult to see the apparent manipulation of the legal system which worked only to the benefit of Mussolini.

Soon after World War Two the global capitalist system began to shape. Capitalism grew to represent the global base structure of the world economy. According to Robinson "the second world war signaled the rise of the transnational fraction among aspiring elites who begin to liaise with the global bourgeoisie and articulate a project for full (re)integration into world capitalism" (Robinson, 75). The base structure of the world economic system today is the capitalism controlled by one dominant social group. According to Robinson this current period of capitalism is distinguishable from earlier ones (Robinson 4). At its core, this global capitalist system while it has undergone dramatic changes over the years it remains true to traditional Marxism's in its oppressive nature. According to Robinson, there remains only distortions of 'subjective consciousness' of nation states (Robinson,

106). He argues that nation-state geographical boundaries only serve as a system to "box in and control populations with fixed physical boundaries so that their labour can be more efficiently exploited and their resistance [to the advancements of capital] contained" (Robinson, 106). In this way nation-states as Gramsci saw them no longer exist, where the interests of the dominant group were contained by boarders. The dominant social group is no longer confined to nation-states but is now identified by Robinson as having global interests and influence.

The same sediment is expressed by Giovanni Arrighi in his book entitled *Adam Smith in Beijing*, who argues that there now exist two groups of dominant social groups fighting for global control. In contrast to Robinsons view of one dominant social group Arrighi argues that there is currently a clash between the West U.S. social group and East Asian social group on a global level. This represents each group attempt to control base structure of the global capitalism system. The Eastern Asian dominant social group has struggled against the U.S. hegemony to take control of the modes of production in the Asia. According to Arrighi this resistance was a culmination of events over the years (Arrighi, 1-2).

> "The resistance has occurred through a snowballing process of connected economic 'miracles' in the succession of east Asian states, starting in Japan in the 1950's and 1960's, rolling on in South Korea, Taiwan, Hong Kong, Singapore, Malaysia, and Thailand in the 1970s and 1980s, and culminating in the 1990s and

> early 2000 in the emergence of China as
> the world's most dynamic center of
> economic and commercial expansion."
> (Arrighi, 2).

This 'snowballing effect' expresses the dynamic or organic transformation of East Asia, still in its 'inchoate phase'. The argument presented by Arrighi is that the Eastern Asian dominant social group "will be no doubt... the most dramatic in terms of its impact on the rest of the world... especially on neighboring countries" (Arrighi, 2). Arrighi's position is that the Eastern hegemony has developed as a counter-hegemonic force to soon dominate over that of the U.S. Western hegemony. The claim by Arrighi assumes that the U.S. hegemonic force was unable to maintain its influence and dominant over the East. To strengthen Arrighi's argument he extends Gramsci's theory of hegemony identifying organized consent to include the threat of physical force. In other words, while the U.S. hegemony expanded over the world soon after World War Two, the Eastern Asian countries only submitted to their influence, following the expansion of capitalism out of fear of reprisals. The threat of force by the U.S. military alone cannot constitute a stable form of leadership in the Gramscian sense.

In contrast, Robinson argues there is only one globally dominant social group. The global dominant social group represents for Robinson the transnational class or TNC or TCC. Transnational because this class is tied to the circuits of production on a global scale (Robinson, 47). This groups according to Robinson, is currently involved in a struggle from within on how to best manage world affairs, under there one global hegemony.

According to Robinson, the US

> "has taken the lead in developing policies and strategies on behalf of the global capitalist agenda precisely because it was the last 'hegemon' among core powers, because globalization emerged in the period of worldwide US dominance, and the concentration of resources and coercive powers within the US national state allows it to play a leadership role on behalf of a transnational elite. Due to the particular manner in which the world economy and the global capitalist relations unfolded in the post war Two period, the US transnationalized. To advance the interests the TCC (TNC) has relied on existing nation-state-apparatuses and, increasingly, on the emergent apparatus of the TNS, and in doing so it has found the US national state to be the most powerful of these apparatuses. This is the particular form through which the old geopolitical of the nation state are simultaneously being played out and winding down" (Robinson 135).

The collective force of this dominant social group leads globally. Therefore, all nation-states consisting of both political and civil societies are all under the same hegemonic control of one dominant ideology.

Both Robinson and Arrighi apply Gramsci's theory of

hegemony in the international context. According to Arrighi by using leadership only in the nation-state context

> "as Gramsci does, an increase in the power of the state vis-à-vis other states is an important component-and in itself a measure-of the successful pursuit of the general (that is-national) interest. But, when we use the term leadership in an international context to designate the fact that a dominant state leads the system of states in a desired direction, the general interest cannot be defined in terms of an increase in the power of an individual state over others, because by definition this power cannot increase for a system as a whole. A general interest for the system as a whole can, nonetheless, be identified by focusing on the collective rather than the distributive aspects of power" (Arrighi, 150).

The theory of hegemony was applied by Gramsci only to the nation-state. The reason was that at the time of Gramsci writing of the *Prison Note Books*, international forces were not influential. According to Gramsci, outside forces actively influencing the nation-state were discussions of 'petty politics' (SPN, 116). He did anticipate the possibility that in the future their might be a consideration of applying his theory in the international context. According to Gramsci "it is true that the conquest of power and achievement of a new productive world are inseparable, and the propaganda for one of them is also propaganda for the other, and in reality, is solely in this coincidence that the unity of the dominant class-at once economic and political-resides" (SPN, 116). This complex relationship "arises of the relation of internal forces in the country in question, of the relation of international forces, of the countries geo-political position" (SPN, 116). Gramsci points out that in the 1930 certain ideological advances had been made by intellectuals of different nation states which only constituted as talk among different influential individuals in regards to different advancements which had been made by industrial countries (SPN, 116-118).

Arrighi avoids the discussion of global culture unlike Robinson who discusses at length the effects on world cultures by the dominant ideology of the transnational class. Robinson explicitly identifies that the dominant ideology of the TCC is working to influence the entire civil institutions of all societies within countries around the world, taking control of both public and private institutions. He makes a point of identifying the most basic of institutional mechanisms that have influenced all cultures around the world. The idea of a global culture for Robinson at its most basic understanding is symbolic. According to Robinson, "a superficially convergent culture emerges in which certain industries-entertainment, fashion, tourism, the visual media, sports, popular music, and the cult of celebrities-are crucial" (Robinson, 31). This represents the corporate capitalist culture, that has influenced cultures world-wide into a new global awareness. This for Arrighi is implied in his discussion of the relationship surrounding the issues of economic competition between the U.S. and Eastern Asian corporations (Arrighi, 144). Arrighi finds that the U.S. hegemony had never had a hold of the political and civil societies on a global scale that soon after World War Two spent more time on containment of communism and the taming of nationalism while unable to integrate its ideological domination in the East (Arrighi, 154). It would be hard to imagine that Arrighi would doubt the influence on Chinese culture, as Robinson identifies, by the corporate capitalist culture. Unlike Robinson, Arrighi remains state-centric in his entire theory while describing collective international forces. The main U.S. hegemony that has its own dominant ideology and the Eastern Asian dominant ideology, each represents a conglomerate of nation-states fighting for control over the global economy and for global hegemony.

Before the theory of hegemony can be applied internationally, Gramsci warns of confusing leadership by a dominant social group with what might only represent the coincidental workings of intellectuals in an international context. Unless the rational of a dominant international social group or groups is clearly united, then there is no hegemony on a global scale. According to Gramsci,

> " one can see how, when the impetus of progresses not tightly linked to a vast local economic development which is artificially limited and repressed, but is instead the reflection of international development which transmits their ideological currents to the periphery-currents born on the basis of the productive development of more advanced countries-then the group which is the bearer of new ideas is not the economic group but the intellectual stratum, and the conception of the State

> advocated by them changes aspect; it is
> conceived of as something in itself, as a
> rational absolute" (SPN, 116-117).

The problem in applying hegemony internationally is in the ability to distinguish a dominant social group or groups from what may be the workings and interactions by a stratum of intellectuals. A criticism of both theorists is the possibility that what is being identified by Robinson and Arrighi are the coincidental interactions between groups of intellectuals working within the global base structure and not collective forces of dominant social groups on an international level in control of the means of production. According to Gramsci the state is only conceivable as a specific system of production, this does not mean that the relationship of means to an end can be easily determined… or is apparent at first sight (SPN, 116). It's entirely possible that what both Robinson and Arrighi are describing as a dominant social group on an international collective sphere, is actually representative of a group of intellectuals whose interests are coincidentally aligned. Using Gramsci's conception of hegemony; for there to be hegemony in the nation-state then there must be a stable form of leadership; and this is constituted by the fact that hegemony is protection of organized consent by the armor of coercion (SPN, 262). Robinson's makes a compelling argument for the flow of transnational capital and the rise of a transnational class. Arrighi's theory that accounts for the rise of Eastern Asian power is equally compelling. The problem is that each theorist failed to address this concern of Gramsci. By addressing this concern, each theory must entertain the possibility there is a need to clarify the coincidental actions by groups of intellectuals engaged in international affairs. Closest that Each theorist has come to touching on this idea is that they reinforce the idea that hegemony is closely tied to capital accumulation. The problem is not that both Arrighi and Robison are incorrect in their theorizations, but that neither address this concern of Gramsci in their application of Gramsci's theory of hegemony in the international context.

Each theory by both Robinson and Arrighi, is based on the conception of a collective force or forces on an international level controlling the global economic system. No nation-state is autonomous in this sense, even under the world-view system of Arrighi. According to Arrighi's thesis,

> "the failure of the Project for a New American century and the success of Chinese economic development, taken jointly, have made the realization of Smith's vision of a world-market society based on greater equality among the world's civilizations more likely than ever was in the almost two and a half centuries since the publication of the Wealth of Nations" (Arrighi, 8).

There may very well be no invisible hand moving market forces as expressed by Smith. Are global markets moved towards an equilibrium by one or two global dominant social groups? The concern has been raised that economic theorists have fail to adequately show what moves international market forces. According to Joseph Stiglitz,

> "is it because economics as a discipline attracts individuals who are, by nature, more selfish, or is it because economics

> helps shape individuals, making them more selfish? The answer, almost certainly, is a little bit of both. Presumably, future experimental research will help resolve the question of the relative importance of these two hypotheses" (Stiglitz, 1).

What the Nobel prize winning theorist Joseph Stiglitz argues is what actually moves international market forces is questionable but in part due to the possession of asymmetrical information between participants in the global markets. For the purposes of this paper the concern is not a question of free markets and their efficiency, but by what this assertion of Stiglitz implies. The implication is that there simply exists an irrationality in the global markets and not a discernable aligned rationality between international economic forces. If markets are a good indication of global economics then this type of observable irrationality is what Gramsci warned about in adopting his theory of hegemony to an international context.

Neither Robinson nor Arrighi by applying Gramsci's theory of hegemony in the international context, have addressed one key concern made by Gramsci. Robinson's argument is compelling in that through the control of TNC, the global financial system etc., there exist an elite social group dominating both the global base structure and soon to be the superstructures of all countries under one hegemony. Similarly, Arrighi's analysis of various economic crisis and U.S. military might, is a compelling argument that supports the rise of the Eastern Asia historic block. The problem is that for there to be international hegemony in the Gramscian sense then there must be global stable leadership consisting of all of the elements within the superstructure. Both institutional forces working towards organized consent, as Gramsci defined them in relation to an identifiable dominant ideology, must be identifiable. Global interests cannot be coincidentally aligned under the illusion created by intellectuals working on a global financial platform. A claim of hegemony in the international context by one or more dominant social groups of other nation states must be substantiated. This must be identified against the global capitalist system as it is known today, that any claim of hegemony is not simply representative of groups of interconnected intellectuals accessing a platform for conducting coincidentally like-minded business. As integrated the global system of capitalism might be; to ignore this implication is to ignore Gramsci's own warning in applying his theory of hegemony internationally. So, to identify hegemony as Gramsci imagined, is to identify all of the institutional elements of the superstructure working under one economic system. supporting one dominant ideology and thus one ruling class. If one of these elemental forces is lacking then there can be no hegemony as a complete system, which is what Gramsci envisioned for the nation state. Talks of hegemonic forces by Gramsci differ from what he envisioned of the hegemony of the ruling class that exists in the nation state.

Conclusion:

The Supreme Court of Canada is active in maintaining organized consent. This example represents the educational role of the court as one of the foundational elements of Gramsci's theory of hegemony. Governments aim is to achieve organic continuity, by finding a balance in interests though coercive tools between subgroups and the interests of the ruling class within the state. This balancing of interests is achieved through the reinforcement of the existing abstract values that are currently supported by the existing level of civilizing within the state. Reinforcing these abstract principles by building upon their interpretations, enables leadership to create new laws and raise levels of civilizing according to their direction. While the majority of everyone may agree that it is wrong to commit an illegal act of killing someone the mass population is also primed to consider that there is something wrong when individuals do not contribute to society by getting up and going to work every day. How can people begin to imagine a nation state where people can peruse interests that are not directed at supporting the modes of productive forces but are the interests of the individual persons own thirst for knowledge and bettering of others, free from economic restraints (free from feeding the economic machine). Individual people can all grow to both realize that they choose not to commit heinous acts against their fellow human being while arriving at a society that is free from the need for money and create a utopian environment. Why have we not achieved this? Different pressures working (often together simultaneously) within both political and civil societies aid in transforming the behaviors and beliefs of subgroups that would otherwise conflict with the interests of the ruling class within the state to maintain consent to the existing hegemony. But, as it was one main goal of this book to point out that it is this legal coercive element of political society that has gone overlooked by most academics in describing Gramsci's theory of hegemony.

By institutionalizing labour, the Canadian nation state has managed over the years to curve the threat to authority that the militancy of labour had posed in the late 1800's. This curve and complacency of labour represents the achievement of the state to maintain organized consent among this subgroup. Labour by consenting to unionization agreed to follow a system of policies, regulations and different laws in support the guidelines created by the state. Union representatives agreed to support these policies and enter into on behalf of labour and agreed to different contractual agreements created through the ADR process that limited labour's ability to organize and legally strike. Most recently the Supreme court's decision that allows labour a constitutionally protected right to strike has not changed this limitation, representing the states use of coercion. Most unionized labour, through the coercion of contractual agreements, is already under obligations to mediation. This legally suppress labour's ability to strike legally. As a result of joint efforts between government and the ruling class, over time labour has been transformed out of their militancy into an organized institution consenting to the legal control mechanisms which have legally restricted their ability to as affectively as from the movements early years disrupt the modes of productive forces within the state.

The reference process, one form of a specific legal coercive tool created and utilized by the state, allows contentious issues presenting difficulty in the government's ability to gain organic continuity to be deflected from the legislatures to the Courts. This allows the legislative body time to adjust to public opinion and further its acts of legal coercion; if necessary, to gain organic continuity. What scholars such as Panitch and Swarts, Michael Mandel and Trevor Farrow have successfully achieved is to point out examples of the dominant forces that are at work within the state and the state's ability to arrive at organic continuity through legal coercive instruments. This critic of the Canadian labour movement has tried to capture the essence of Gramsci's thoughts. Gramsci's conviction was that

> ideas are not born of other ideas,
> philosophies of other philosophies; they
> are a continually renewed expression of
> real historical development. The unity of
> history (what the idealists call unity of
> spirit) is not a presupposition, but a
> continuously developing process.
> Identity in concrete reality determines
> identity of thought, and not vice versa
> (SPN, 201).

It is here, in this quote, that Gramsci seems to show his delight in the Aristotelian tradition in how the practicality of rigorous thought aids in current real-world applications. Hegemony is a nation state concept developed by Gramsci where all of the elements, which must include the level of civilizing by the law and the educative function of the courts, that must be incorporated into any consideration or understanding of what hegemony. Without the law and the educative forces of the courts as an institution, there is no hegemony as Gramsci had meant it to mean and be understood. Theorist who base their ideas of a global hegemony must rethink their analysis and re-consider what Gramsci meant by hegemony as a nation state before they begin to apply his ideas on a broader scale.

Bibliography:

Albert, Richard, *How Unwritten Constitutional Norms Change Written Constitutions*,
> http://lawdigitalcommons.bc.edu/cgi/viewcontent.cgi?article=1982&context=lsfp (7/11/2017)

Arrighi, Giovanni *Adam Smith In Beijing*. Verso; London-New York 2007

Black's law Dictionary Continental Edition (1891-1991)

Baschiera, Marianela *An Introduction to the Italian Legal System. The Allocation of Normative Powers*
> http://scholarship.law.cornell.edu/cgi/viewcontent.cgi?article=1059&context=ijli (7/11/2017)

Carissima, Mathen *Dialogue Theory, Judicial Review, and Judicial Supremacy: A Comment on "Charter Dialogue Revised*
> http://digitalcommons.osgoode.yorku.ca/cgi/viewcontent.cgi?article=1258&context=ohlj (7/11/2017)

Cristea, Ioana *Antonio Gramsci's Concept of Ideology*
> http://seejps.lumina.org/index.php/volume-i-number-3-ideologies-and-patterns-of-democracy/49-antonio-gramsci-s-concept-of-ideology#_ftn20 (7/11/2017)

Dodek, Adam., *Courting Constitutional Danger: Constitutional Conventions and the Legacy of the Patriation Reference,* Supreme Court Law Review (2011), 54 S.C.L.R. (2d)

Gill, Stephen and Law, David., *Global Hegemony and the Structural Power of Capital* 1989
https://people.ucsc.edu/~rlipsch/migrated/Pol17/Gill%20and%20Law.pdf (7/11/2017)

Gottleb, Roger S. *An Anthology of Western Marxism*
http://www.csun.edu/~snk1966/Gramsci%20-%20Prison%20Notebooks%20-%20Intellectuals.pdf (7/11/2017)

Government of Canada website referenced at
http://www.scc-csc.ca/court-cour/judges-juges/spe-dis/bm-2004-11-22-eng.aspx

Gramsci, Antonio *Prison Notebooks*. International publishers; New York 2012

Harder, Douglas Wilhelm *The History of Common Law in Canada Tort Law and Professional Engineering Intellectual Property*
https://ece.uwaterloo.ca/~dwharder/epel/Lecture_materials/ECE.290.pdf, (7/11/2017)

Hunt, Allen *Rights and Social Movements: Counter Hegemonic strategies*, Journal of Law and Society Vol 17, No 3 Cardiff University 1990

Huscroft, Grant, *Politics and the Reference Power*
http://www.cpsa-acsp.ca/papers-2010/Huscroft.pdf(7/11/2017)

Judicial Committee act 1833,
> http://ozcase.library.qut.edu.au/qhlc/documents/qr_privy_judicial_1833_3-4_Wm4_c41.pdf
(7/11/2017)

Kennedy, Duncan *Antonio Gramsci and the Legal System*
> http://duncankennedy.net/documents/Photo%20articles/Antonio%20Gramsci%20and%20The%20Legal%20System.pdf (7/11/2017)

Litowitz, Douglas *Gramsci, Hegemony, and the Law*
> http://digitalcommons.law.byu.edu/cgi/viewcontent.cgi?article=1992&context=lawreview
(7/11/2017)

Lokan, Andrew and Dassios, Christopher, *Constitutional Litigation in Canada* Toronto:
> Thomson Reuters Canada Limited 2006

Mandel, Ernest *The Leninist Theory of Organization*
> https://www.ernestmandel.org/en/works/txt/1970/leninist_theory_organisation.htm (7/12/2017)

Mandel, Michael, The Charter of Rights and the Legalization of politics in Canada. Copyright 1994 Thompson Publishing.

Peraud, Radakrishnan, THE ROLE OF JUDICIAL ADVISORY OPINIONS IN CANADIAN CONSTITUTIONALISM AND FEDERALISM: THE SENATE, PATRIATION & QUEBEC VETO REFERENCE CASES CONSIDERED.

http://www.collectionscanada.gc.ca/obj/s4/f2/dsk2/tape15/PQDD_0012/NQ31948.pdf

Puddster, Kate., Unraveling Reference Questions: Theoretical and Political Implications in a
 Canadian Context. http://www.cpsa-acsp.ca/papers-2013/Puddister.pdf
 (7/11/2017)

Rand, Hon. Ivan C., The Supreme Court of Canada
 http://robsonhall.ca/mlj/sites/default/files/articles/the%20supreme%20court%20of%20canada.pdf
 (7/11/2017)

Riley, Dylan J *Hegemony and Democracy in Gramsci's Prison Notebooks*
 http://sociology.berkeley.edu/sites/default/files/faculty/Riley/hegemonydemocracy.pdf
 (7/11/2017)

Roach, Kent, *The Supreme Court On Trial: Judicial Activism Or Democratic Dialogue*.
 Irwin Law A Quicklaw Company, pub 2001.

Robinson, William I *A Theory of Global capitalism*: Production, *Class, and State in a
 Transnational World*. The Johns Hopkins University Press; Baltimore London 2004

Rubin, Gerald, *The Nature, Use and Effect of Reference Cases in Canadian Constitutional Law*.
 http://lawjournal.mcgill.ca/userfiles/other/7455946-rubin.pdf (7/11/2017)

Russell, Peter., The Patriation and Quebec Veto References: The Supreme Court Wrestles with the Political Part of the Constitution

http://sclr.journals.yorku.ca/index.php/sclr/article/viewFile/34629/31489

Stiglitz, Joseph *There is No Invisible Hand*; An article from the guardian online newspaper
    https://www.theguardian.com/education/2002/dec/20/highereducation.uk1. (7/11/2017),

Strayer, Barry L, *The Canadian Constitution and the Courts: The function and the Scope of*
    Judicial Review, 3rd ed. Toronto: Butterworths, 1988

Trudeau, Pierre,
    http://www.cbc.ca/archives/entry/trudeau-supports-miners-in-the-1957-murdochville-strike (07/07/2017)

Cristea, Ioana *Antonio Gramsci's Concept of Ideology*
    http://seejps.lumina.org/index.php/volume-i-number-3-ideologies-and-patterns-of-democracy/49-antonio-gramsci-s-concept-of-ideology#_ftn20 (7/11/2017)

Cases Cited:

BCE Inc. v. 1976 Debenture holders (2008) referenced from Lexum at:
   https://scc-csc.lexum.com/scc-csc/scc-csc/en/item/6238/index.do (7/11/2017)

Union Carbide Canada Inc. v. Bombardier Inc., 2014 SCC 35 referenced from Lexum at:
   https://scc-csc.lexum.com/scc-csc/scc-csc/en/item/13632/index.do (7/11/2017)

Marriage reference 2004 SCC referenced from Lexum at:
   https://scc-csc.lexum.com/scc-csc/scc-csc/en/item/2196/index.do (7/11/2017)

Ontario (Attorney General) v. Fraser 2011 SCC referenced from Lexum at:
   https://scc-csc.lexum.com/scc-csc/scc-csc/en/item/7934/index.do (7/11/2017)

Patriation reference case 1981 SCC referenced from Lexum at:
   https://   scc-csc.lexum.com/scc-csc/scc-csc/en/item/2519/index.do (7/11/2017)

Succession Reference Quebec, 2105 Supreme Court judgement referenced from Lexum at:
   https://scc-csc.lexum.com/scc-csc/scc-csc/en/item/1643/index.do (7/11/2017)

Saskatchewan Federation of Labour v. Saskatchewan, 2015 SCC, referenced from Lexum

at: https://scc-csc.lexum.com/scc-csc/scc-csc/en/item/14610/index.do (7/11/2017)

Ontario (Attorney General) v. Fraser 2011 referenced at Lexum at:
https://scc-csc.lexum.com/scc-csc/scc-csc/en/item/7934/index.do (7/11/2017)

ABOUT THE AUTHOR

This adventure began as my Master's Thesis for the political science department at York University in Toronto, Canada. I plan on editing this book further but chose to release this version first, feeling the need to share this with the world, sooner than later. The aim is to show the world the brilliance of Gramsci's theory of hegemony in a new light, knowing that new applications of his theory will emerge from the shock that this book will bring to not only the academic world but how it will open dialogue among all of those who read this book. This is a foundational and a must read book, not just for those who love Gramsci or for philosophers, historians, legal scholars etc. but to all of those who have a thirst for knowledge. Hope you enjoy this fascinating journey as much as I did, good reading.

www.ingramcontent.com/pod-product-compliance
Lightning Source LLC
Chambersburg PA
CBHW020418230426
43663CB00007BA/1218